LANGUAGE ARTS
INSTANT ASSESSMENTS
for Data Tracking
Grade 4

Credits
Author: Kristina L. Biddle, M.Ed., NBCT

Visit *carsondellosa.com* for correlations to Common Core, state, national, and Canadian provincial standards.

Carson-Dellosa Publishing, LLC
PO Box 35665
Greensboro, NC 27425 USA
carsondellosa.com

978-1-4838-3619-5
01-339161151

✦ Table of Contents ✦

✦ Assessment and Data Tracking ✦

Data tracking is an essential element in modern classrooms. Teachers are often required to capture student learning through both formative and summative assessments. They then must use the results to guide teaching, remediation, and lesson planning and provide feedback to students, parents, and administrators. Because time is always at a premium in the classroom, it is vital that teachers have the assessments they need at their fingertips. The assessments need to be suited to the skill be assessed as well as adapted to the stage in the learning process. This is true for an informal checkup at the end of a lesson or a formal assessment at the end of a unit.

This book will provide the tools and assessments needed to determine your students' level of mastery throughout the school year. The assessments are both formal and informal and include a variety of formats—pretests and posttests, flash cards, prompt cards, traditional tests, and exit tickets. Often, there are several assessment options for a single skill or concept to allow you the greatest flexibility when assessing understanding. Simply select the assessment that best fits your needs, or use them all to create a comprehensive set of assessments for before, during, and after learning.

Incorporate Instant Assessments into your daily plans to streamline the data-tracking process and keep the focus on student mastery and growth.

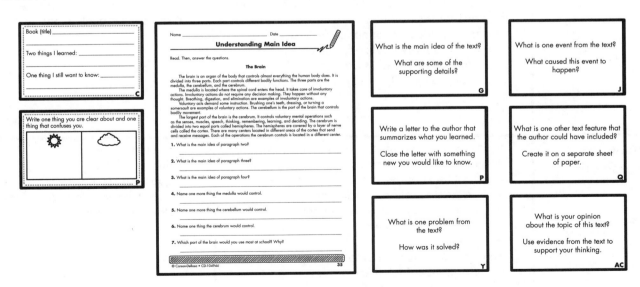

A variety of instant assessments for informational text comprehension

Types of Assessment

Assessment usually has a negative association because it brings to mind tedious pencil-and-paper tests and grading. However, it can take on many different forms and be a positive, integral part of the year. Not all assessments need to be formal, nor do they all need to be graded. Choose the type of assessment to use based on the information you need to gather. Then, you can decide if or how it should be graded.

	What Does It Look Like?	Examples
Formative Assessment	• occurs during learning • is administered frequently • is usually informal and not graded • identifies areas of improvement • provides immediate feedback so a student can make adjustments promptly, if needed • allows teachers to rethink strategies, lesson content, etc., based on current student performance • is process-focused • has the most impact on a student's performance	• in-class observations • exit tickets • reflections and journaling • homework • student-teacher conferences • student self-evaluations
Interim Assessment	• occurs occasionally • is more formal and usually graded • feedback is not immediate, though still fairly quick • helps teachers identify gaps in teaching and areas for remediation • often includes performance assessments, which are individualized, authentic, and performance-based in order to evaluate higher-level thinking skills	• in-class observations • exit tickets • reflections and journaling • homework • student-teacher conferences • student self-evaluations
Summative Assessment	• occurs once learning is considered complete • the information is used by the teacher and school for broader purposes • takes time to return a grade or score • can be used to compare a student's performance to others • is product-focused • has the least impact on a student's performance since there are few or no opportunities for retesting	• cumulative projects • final portfolios • quarterly testing • end-of-the-year testing • standardized testing

How to Use This Book

The assessments in this book follow a few different formats, depending on the skill or concept being assessed. Use the descriptions below to familiarize yourself with each unique format and get the most out of Instant Assessments all year long.

Show What You Know

Most anchors begin with two *Show What You Know* tests. They follow the same format with the same types of questions, so they can be used as a pretest and posttest that can be directly compared to show growth. Or, use one as a test at the end of a unit and use the second version as a retest for students after remediation.

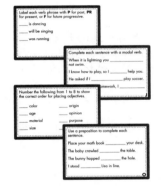

Exit Tickets

Most anchors end with exit tickets that cover the variety of concepts within the anchor. Exit tickets are very targeted questions designed to assess understanding of specific skills, so they are ideal formative assessments to use at the end of a lesson. Exit tickets do not have space for student names, allowing teachers to gather information on the entire class without placing pressure on individual students. If desired, have students write their names or initials on the back of the tickets. Other uses for exit tickets include the following:

- Use the back of each ticket for longer answers, fuller explanations, or extension questions. If needed, students can staple them to larger sheets of paper.
- They can also be used for warm-ups or to find out what students know before a lesson.
- Use the generic exit tickets on pages 7 and 8 for any concept you want to assess. Be sure to fill in any blanks before copying.
- Laminate them and place them in a language arts center as task cards.
- Use them to play Scoot or a similar review game at the end of a unit.
- Choose several to create a targeted assessment for a skill or set of skills.

Word Lists

Word lists consist of several collections of grade-appropriate words in areas that students need to be assessed in, such as sight words, spelling patterns, and words with affixes. They are not comprehensive but are intended to make creating your own assessments simpler. Use the word lists to create vocabulary tests, word decoding fluency tests, spelling lists, etc., for the year.

Cards

Use the cards as prompts for one-on-one conferencing. Simply copy the cards, cut them apart, and follow the directions preceding each set of cards. Use the lettering to keep track of which cards a student has interacted with.

- Copy on card stock and/or laminate for durability.
- Punch holes in the top left corners and place the cards on a book ring to make them easily accessible.
- Copy the sets on different colors of paper to keep them easily separated or to distinguish different sections within a set of cards.
- Easily differentiate by using different amounts or levels of cards to assess a student.
- Write the answers on the backs of cards to create self-checking flash cards.
- Place them in a language arts center as task cards or matching activities.
- Use them to play Scoot or a similar review game at the end of a unit.

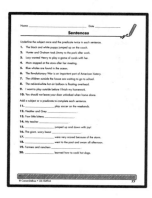

Assessment Pages

The reproducible assessment pages are intended for use as a standard test of a skill. Use them in conjunction with other types of assessment to get a full picture of a student's level of understanding. They can also be used for review or homework.

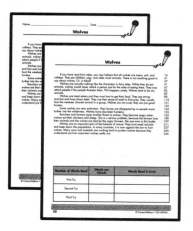

Fluency Pages

Use the paired fluency pages to assess students' oral reading fluency. Provide a copy of the student page to the student, and use the teacher copy to track how far the student read, which words he or she struggled with, and the student's performance on repeated readings. The word count is provided at the end of each line for easy totaling. Then, use the related comprehension questions to assess the student's understanding of what he or she read.

Exit Tickets

Exit tickets are a useful formative assessment tool that you can easily work into your day. You can choose to use a single exit ticket at the end of the day or at the end of each lesson. Simply choose a ticket below and make one copy for each student. Then, have students complete the prompt and present them to you as their ticket out of the door. Use the student responses to gauge overall learning, create small remediation groups, or target areas for reteaching. A blank exit ticket is included on page 8 so you can create your own exit tickets as well.

What stuck with you today?	**List three facts you learned today. Put them in order from most important to least important.** 1. _____ 2. _____ 3. _____
The first thing I'll tell my family about today is	**The most important thing I learned today is**
Color the face that shows how you feel about understanding today's lesson. ☺ ☺ ☹ Explain why. _____	**Summarize today's lesson in 10 words or less.**

One example of _____ is _____
_____
_____
_____
_____ .

One question I still have is _____
_____
_____
_____
_____
_____ .

How will understanding _____
_____
help you in real life? _____
_____
_____
_____

One new word I learned today is
_____ .
It means _____
_____
_____
_____ .

Draw a picture related to the lesson. Add a caption.

_____
_____

If today's lesson were a song, the title would be _____
_____
because _____
_____
_____ .

The answer is _____ .
What is the question? _____
_____
_____
_____
_____
_____

✦ Show What You Know ✦
Reading: Literature

Read. Then, answer the questions.

Henry's Bike

Every kid on Henry's block had a bike. Henry wanted one too. He watched his friends ride off to the park. They waved and asked him to join them. He waved back. It was five blocks to the park. Walking was so slow that by the time he got there, it would be time to go home.

One night, Henry asked his mother for a bike for his birthday. His mother explained that they did not have enough money. Henry went to his room. How would he ever get a bike? Just then, he remembered his teacher saying, "Where there's a will, there's a way."

The next day Henry saw Mrs. Wagner pulling weeds. She was an older woman, so he asked if she needed help. She said yes and sent him to the shed to get gloves. When he opened the door, Henry saw a bike. It was old and the tires were flat, but it looked beautiful to him!

Mrs. Wagner told Henry that it had belonged to her son and asked him if he liked it. She told him that when they finished she would give him a cool glass of lemonade—and the bike! How could he have dreamed that Mrs. Wagner would give him such a **fine** gift for such a little favor?

1. What is the point of view in this story? Circle the words in the story that support your answer.

_____

2. Why did the bike look beautiful to Henry?_____

_____

3. How would you describe Henry? Use evidence from the story to support your answer.

_____

4. Underline the adage in the text. What does it mean? _____

_____

5. What is a synonym for **fine**, as it is used in this story? _____

_____

6. What is the theme of the story? _____

_____

✦ Show What You Know ✦
Reading: Literature

Read. Then, answer the questions.

Rusty

Rusty was a dirty mutt. His once-white hair was gray and brown with **grime**. He wore a black collar around his neck that once was blue. On the collar hung an identification tag—if anyone could get close enough to read it.

Right now, Rusty was on his belly. He inched forward under the lilac bushes. His long hair dragged in the dirt. His bright, black eyes were glued to a plate on the edge of the table. On it was a hamburger. His moist, black nose twitched with the smell. He knew he would get a stern scolding or spray with the hose if the lady of the house caught him in the yard again.

His empty belly made him brave. The screen door slammed as the lady went back for the rest of her goodies. Rusty knew it was time. He flew like a bullet to the edge of the table. The corner of the plate was in his mouth long enough to drop it to the ground. Rusty's mouth seized the burger. The door slammed and a yell was heard. As he dove through a hole in the bushes, water from the hose whitened the back half of his body and his dirty tail.

1. What is the point of view in this story? Circle the words in the story that support your answer.

_____

2. Why did Rusty's nose twitch with the smell?_____

_____

3. How would you describe Rusty? Use evidence from the story to support your answer.

_____

_____

_____

4. Underline the simile in the text. What does it mean? _____

_____

5. What is a synonym for **grime**, as it is used in this story? _____

_____

6. What is the theme of the story? _____

_____

Literature Text
Comprehension Prompts

Use the following cards to assess students' comprehension of fiction texts. You may choose to ask students the questions orally before, during, and after reading. Or, you can give students a card and ask them to respond in writing. Additionally, you may choose to use several cards to create an impromptu assessment for a text. Use cards A–D for before reading, cards E–M for during reading, and cards N–AD for after reading.

Look at the cover of the book and read the title. Make a prediction about the text. **A**	Read the short summary on the back cover. Make a prediction about the text. **B**
Skim through the text. Make a prediction about what will happen. **C**	Look at the front and back covers and skim the pages. Which genre do you think this is? Why? **D**
As you are reading, write at least two things you are wondering about. **E**	Who are the main characters? Use three words to describe each main character and give text evidence to support your choices. **F**

Describe an event from the story.

How did the main character react to this event?

G

What is the setting of the story?

How does the setting impact the story?

H

Who are the characters in the story?

Who is the main character?

Who are the supporting characters?

I

Name an event from the story.

How did each character react to the event?

J

Write an acrostic poem about the main character.

K

Who is the main character?

Would you want to be friends with him or her?

Why or why not?

L

Based upon everything you've read so far, what do you think will happen next?

Why do you think this?

M

What are some words from the story that are important?

Explain why each word is important.

N

Who is the narrator?
Name one other character
in the story.

How would the story be
different if it was told from that
character's point of view?

O

If you were going to give the
author a grade for this story, what
grade would you give him or her?

Why?

P

Pretend that you are
the main character.

If you were writing a
journal about your day,
what might you write about?

Q

Think about the problem
in the story.

If you were giving advice
to the main character, what
advice could you give them?

R

How would the story be different
if a different character from the
story was the main character?

S

From which point of view
is this story written?

What evidence do you have?

T

Draw a picture that shows
what the story means to you.

U

How is the text organized?

How do you know?

V

Pretend to be the main character. Finish the following sentences.

I want _____ .

I wonder _____ .

I understand _____ .

I like _____ .

I try _____ .

W

Pretend to be the main character. Finish the following sentences.

I say _____ .

I see _____ .

I touch _____ .

I hear _____ .

I feel _____ .

X

Pretend to be the main character. Finish the following sentences.

I worry _____ .

I dream _____ .

I pretend _____ .

I cry _____ .

I laugh _____ .

Y

Summarize the story.

Z

How did the main character change from the beginning of the story to the end?

What caused this change?

AA

Create a billboard trying to convince your classmates to read the story.

AB

Create a comic strip that summarizes the story.

AC

List one connection you have to the text.

How did this connection help you better understand the story?

AD

Character Analysis

Read. Then, answer the questions.

Neighbors Need Neighbors

There was an old lady who lived on the edge of town. Everyone referred to her as Granny. Because she kept to herself, she seemed a little different to some. She asked nothing of anyone and did nothing for anyone, except her many dogs. The number of dogs varied daily. Some only came when they were hungry and then left until they returned to eat again. Some knew a good home when they saw it and stayed.

One day, the paper boy noticed Granny's papers had not been picked up for three or four days. The dogs in her yard were thin and moved about slowly. He had not seen Granny for about a week. He wondered if she was all right.

He got off his bike and walked up the steps onto the front porch. He walked around and peered in the windows, but he did not see anything. He opened the front door slightly and called, "Hello! Anyone here?" He listened for a minute. He thought he heard a whimpering sound, so he quickly rode to the closest neighbor's house and called 9-1-1.

When the police arrived, they found Granny had fallen and had not been able to move to call for help. The paramedics said that Granny needed to go to the hospital where she stayed for a few days.

While she was in the hospital, the paper boy came to feed her dogs every day. When Granny came home, neighbors brought food and flowers. Granny was sorry she had not gotten to know her new friends sooner, but was glad she had now "found" them.

1. Describe Granny at the beginning of the story.

_____

_____

2. Describe the paper boy.

_____

_____

3. How did Granny change from the beginning of the story to the end?

_____

_____

4. What caused Granny to change?

_____

Making Inferences

Read. Then, answer the questions.

Jessica's New Room

School was going to begin, and Jessica had mixed feelings about the fourth grade. Her older sister had spent the summer warning Jessica about the dangers of fourth grade.

One day, Jessica got an idea. She needed a fourth-grader's bedroom. Jessica's room had many reminders of her early school years. She needed a more grown-up-looking room. She gathered some magazines with decorating tips and walked to her mother's basement office. She knew her mother liked well-thought-out ideas and presentations, so she prepared her thoughts on the way.

She found her mother and explained that she was very excited about being a **top-notch** fourth grader. Then, she went on to say that for this to happen, she needed a change.

Jessica placed several magazines on the table and explained that she was no longer a baby. She showed some pictures of older-looking bedroom styles, and her mother looked at each one carefully.

Her mother smiled and told her that it was a great idea. For almost an hour, Jessica and her mother swapped ideas and planned her new room.

Jessica was excited about the change for her old room and was certain this would help make her year in the fourth grade a good one.

1. What dangers do you think Jessica's sister is talking about?

_____

_____

2. Why do you think Jessica wanted a new room?

_____

_____

3. What types of things do you think are in Jessica's room now?

_____

_____

4. What do you think **top-notch** means? Use evidence from the text to support your inference.

_____

_____

Story Elements

Read. Then, answer the questions.

The Shortcut

We probably should have taken the road home from the baseball park. It was getting dark, though, and we decided to take the shortcut home. I was the oldest and should have made a better choice.

The shortcut from the baseball park to home was along the railroad tracks. After Roberto's game was over, we were excited. The game had gone into extra innings and Roberto's team had won! Maria and little Carmon were running to keep up while they chewed on their candy necklaces. When we came to the turn for the shortcut, we were so excited and happy that we just took it. We should have stayed on the road.

We walked for about five minutes on the tracks. The sides were steep, and there were thick branches and murky water at the bottom. Maria asked how we would know if a train was coming. I said that we would feel the tracks rumbling.

It was then that I heard the train whistle far away. You never can tell when a train will come through. I did not want to worry the little ones, so I calmly said, "Let's go back to the road." We turned around, and I walked pretty fast. Everyone followed.

Soon, we felt the tracks rumbling, and I shouted, "Run!" I grabbed little Carmon in my arms, and Roberto held Maria's hand. We ran as fast as we could. Then I could see the headlights, and the train blew its loud whistle. We kept running, and I shouted, "Get off the tracks, NOW!" We jumped off the tracks. We all slid down the side, trying hard to stay out of the scratchy bushes. Maria and Carmon were crying but I could not hear them. The loud train was rushing by us.

After the train went by, we climbed back up the hill. We were all scratched up from the bushes, but no one complained. We were all shaking as we walked back to the road. We knew we would never take the shortcut home again.

1. What makes the setting important?

_____

2. What lesson does the author want the reader to learn?

_____

3. Who do you think the narrator is? Underline evidence to support your answer.

_____

4. Describe the narrator. Use evidence from the story to support your answer.

_____

_____

Literature Comprehension

Read. Then, answer the questions.

David's Secret

David and Connor were excited because they were going to the beach. David had never been to a beach before.

Connor told David all about the paddleboat. "I like to paddle to the deep part and then jump in the water," Connor said. David felt butterflies in his stomach. He did not know how to swim. He didn't know Connor was so brave.

At the beach, the boys played in the water, jumping in the waves and laughing. David thought the beach was great!

Then, Connor's dad called them over to the boat dock. He had the paddleboat ready for them and held two life jackets in his hands. David was very nervous. Connor's dad helped him put on his life jacket. David put his feet on the pedals. Connor started paddling, so David did also. Soon, they were moving quickly across the water. It was fun! When they were far out in the lake, Connor stopped the boat and jumped in the water. David was as still as a statue. He did not dare tell Connor that he couldn't swim. Would Connor laugh at him?

Connor watched David and guessed what was wrong. He climbed back onto the boat. "Do you know how to swim?" he asked kindly. David shook his head. Connor smiled at his friend and said, "Let's paddle around some more. Then, after lunch, I'll teach you a little about swimming." David smiled at his best friend. Why had he ever worried about telling Connor that he did not know how to swim?

1. What is the theme of the story?

_____

2. What best shows that Connor is a good friend?

_____

_____

3. Underline one example of figurative language in the story. Tell what type it is and explain what it means.

_____

_____

4. How does the setting affect the story?

_____

_____

Using Text Evidence

Read. Then, answer the questions.

Mystery of the Disappearing Lunches

As soon as we were old enough, we became responsible for packing our own lunches. My five brothers made all of their lunches, and I did too. But, having five brothers in the kitchen in the morning was chaos! I started making my lunch the night before when it was calm and quiet.

One Sunday night, I made my favorite lunch and stored it in a bag in the refrigerator. When I went to grab it Monday morning, it was gone! Mom asked all of my brothers, but each one denied taking my lunch.

I would have let it go, but the next morning my lunch was missing again! Every day for a week, I had to make lunch **on the fly** because the one I prepared the night before was gone.

My brothers can be annoying sometimes, but they are always honest. Mom wanted to believe them, but she also wanted to find out what was happening. That night, she brought it up at the dinner table. She told Dad about everything so that he could help solve the problem.

Dad began to blush. He cleared his throat and said, "Oh, those lunches weren't for me? I thought you were saving me time by packing my lunch, since I've been going to work at five in the morning." Who could have guessed that Dad was the culprit? Our mouths dropped open in shock and then we all started laughing!

The mystery of my missing lunches was solved. Mom offered to make Dad lunch on the days he worked overtime, and my brothers were off the hook!

1. What is the point of view of this story? Circle the words in the story that support your answer.

_____

2. What does **on the fly** mean? How do you know?

_____

_____

3. What does Mom do when she thinks something is wrong?

_____

_____

4. What is the theme of the story? Use text evidence in your answer.

_____

_____

_____

_____

Comparing and Contrasting Texts

Read. Then, answer the questions.

The Fox and the Crow

A crow sat in a tree with a piece of cheese it had just taken from an open window. A fox who was walking by saw the crow and wanted the cheese.

"Good day, Miss Crow," he cried. "You are looking beautiful today. Your feathers are very glossy. Your eyes are shining brightly. I have heard that your voice **surpasses** that of all the other birds. Please, let me hear one song from you so that I may call you the Queen of Birds."

Crow lifted up her head and began to caw her best, but the moment she opened her mouth, the piece of cheese fell to the ground. The cheese was immediately snapped up by Fox.

The Dog and the Bone

A dog was walking over a bridge carrying a bone. The dog looked into the stream and saw another dog carrying a bigger bone. The dog jumped into the water because he wanted the bigger bone. But, in doing so, he dropped his bone. There was no other bone.

1. How are these stories alike?

_____

_____

2. How are these stories different?

_____

_____

3. Describe Fox. Use evidence from the story.

_____

_____

4. How do you think Crow felt after she sang her song? Why?

_____

_____

5. What does **surpass** mean?

_____

Describing Characters

Read. Then, answer the questions.

Rise and Shine

"Rise and shine, Trey," Mrs. Walker said as she gazed down at the lump in the bed. "Today is a big day!"

The lump did not move. Mrs. Walker leaned over and shook the bed. A groan came from beneath the covers. Trey crawled out from under them.

Mrs. Walker approached the second bed. "Wake up, Owen! Summer is over. No more sleeping late." A head slowly peeked out, followed by the rest of a disheveled body.

"Be downstairs in 10 minutes," the boys' mother instructed.

Trey went into the bathroom and turned on the water. "Thith will be a thuper year," he said. A toothbrush stuck out from his mouth.

"What?" Owen asked. He changed out of his pajamas and into blue jeans. He heard Trey spit into the sink.

"This will be a super year," Trey repeated. "New classes, new teachers, and a junior basketball team!" He winked at Owen.

"I'm a little nervous," Owen admitted. "I'm new at this, you know."

"Oh, middle school takes a little bit of getting used to," Trey agreed. "But, after a few days it will feel like you've been there forever! Remember, I had to go through it last year."

"Oh, so now that you're a big seventh grader you run the school?" Owen teased.

"Just don't do anything to embarrass me," Trey smiled back.

"You mean like tell everyone you think Lily Kim is the prettiest girl in the school?"

Trey blushed. Just then, some wonderful smells wafted in. Both boys stopped and inhaled deeply.

"Race you downstairs!" Owen shouted.

1. Describe how Trey is feeling. Why is he feeling this way?

_____

2. Describe how Owen is feeling. Why is he feeling this way?

_____

3. Describe Owen and Trey's relationship.

_____

4. How do the boys change from the beginning of the story to the end?

_____

_____

Elements of Poetry

Read. Then, answer the questions.

Shadow March (from North-West Passage)
by Robert Louis Stevenson

All round the house is the jet-black night;
It stares through the window-pane;
It crawls in the corners, hiding from the light
And it moves with the moving flame.

Now my little heart goes a-beating like a drum,
With the breath of the Bogie in my hair,
And all round the candle the crooked shadows come,
And go marching along up the stair.

The shadows of the balusters, the shadow of the lamp,
The shadow of the child that goes to bed—
All the wicked shadows coming tramp, tramp, tramp,
With the black night overhead.

1. How does the author feel about the shadows? How do you know?

_____

_____

2. Underline an example of figurative language in the poem. What type is it? How do you know?

_____

_____

3. What was the author's purpose in including the figurative language?

_____

_____

4. Label the structural elements of the poem.

5. The author gives the shadows human characteristics. What effect does this have on the reader?

_____

_____

A

Theme

Supporting Detail	Supporting Detail

B

Title _____

_____

Genre _____

I know this because _____

_____

_____ .

C

Title _____

_____

Point of View _____

_____

I know this because _____

_____ .

D

Write **P** for poetry, **PR** for prose, or **D** for drama next to each structural element.

_____ cast   _____ stage directions

_____ stanza   _____ meter

_____ rhythm   _____ setting

_____ paragraph   _____ theme

_____ dialogue   _____ chapter

E

Describe the setting of the story.

_____

_____

How would the story be different with another setting?

_____

_____

F

Title _____

Summary _____

_____

_____

Would you recommend this story to a friend?

yes   **no**

G

New Word	Definition
Strategy	**How It Helped**

H

Title _____

Example of figurative language _____

_____

Type _____

Meaning _____

_____

Pretend you are the main character. "Update" your social media status to show what happened to you.

_____
_____
_____
_____

I

Write a social media post that captures the main idea of the story. Include a hashtag and keep it to less than 150 characters.

_____
_____
_____
_____

J

One connection I made to the text:

_____
_____

How it helped me understand the story:

_____
_____

K

Title: _____

1 I struggled to read it.

2 I could read it with help.

3 It was just right.

4 It was too easy.

L

Describe what you think will happen next.

_____
_____
_____
_____
_____

M

Think about the story and fill in the chart.

Cause	Effect

N

Which comprehension strategy did you use today?

_____
_____

How did it help?

_____
_____

O

Write one question about the story.

_____
_____

Switch tickets with a friend and answer each other's question.

_____
_____

P

✦ Show What You Know ✦
Reading: Informational Text

Read. Then, answer the questions.

Home Sweet Home

For thousands of years, people have lived on the Great Plains of the United States and Canada. The Great Plains is a huge expanse of flat, grassy land with few trees. Many different animals used to roam on the plains. The groups of people who lived there would travel around and follow the animals to hunt. **They needed homes that they could tear down** and set up fairly quickly. Many Plains tribes, such as the Blackfoot, Sioux, and Cheyenne, built tipis to use as homes.

The first step in making a tipi was to find and prepare the poles. It took 15 poles to make just one tipi. The poles for the frame had to be long and straight. The best trees for this purpose were willow, pine, and cedar. The branches and bark were cut off so they did not poke holes in the tipi cover. When the people traveled with their homes, the poles dragged on the ground. The poles wore out and had to be replaced every year or two.

To prepare the buffalo hides, the women worked together on many steps. First, they scraped and cleaned the inside and outside of each hide. Then, they soaked the hides with water to soften them. Next, they sewed as many as 14 hides together in the shape of a half circle. They cut a hole for the door and created smoke flaps. Finally, they fitted the cover over the frame and lit a fire inside. The smoke from the fire helped to preserve the skins. Some tipis were decorated with designs and symbols.

In the late 1800s, life on the plains changed a lot. Many roads and cities began to fill the area. The buffalo were almost all gone. Many of the Plains people were forced to live on reservations. They no longer lived in tipis. Still, the tipi remains an important part of Native American culture today.

1. What is the main idea of the text? _____

_____

2. List at least two details that support the main idea.

_____

_____

3. What is the meaning of the phrase **they needed homes that they could tear down**?

_____

_____

4. Why do you think willow, pine, and cedar trees were the best to use?

_____

✦ Show What You Know ✦
Reading: Informational Text

Read. Then, answer the questions.

The *Mayflower*

Imagine leaving behind your home and all of your things. Imagine sailing across the ocean to a new world where there are no towns and no homes. This is what the passengers of the *Mayflower* faced on their journey from England to America in 1620.

The *Mayflower* traveled for 66 days across the unpredictable Atlantic Ocean. The ship carried 102 passengers and nearly 30 crew members. The passengers were the people who were traveling on the boat from England to America. The sailors, or crew, were the people who worked on the ship. The crew planned to return to England once the passengers were settled.

Travel was difficult in rough weather. Passengers ate oatmeal, hard biscuits, dried fruit, rice, and salted beef brought with them from England. Many of the passengers became seasick during the trip. Occasionally, when the weather was calm, they would go up on deck to get fresh air and stretch their legs. The sailors preferred them to stay belowdecks and out of their way.

Every sailor was busy with the job of maintaining the ship. Some sailors climbed high on the mast to the lookout. Others put the sails up or down and repaired torn sails. Some sailors steered the boat. Others cooked for the crew. Many of the sailors helped to keep the boat clean. The sailors were paid well.

When the ship landed in the Plymouth harbor, the passengers started **the difficult task of settling in**. They needed to build homes and get ready for the coming winter. Even the children had to work hard. As soon as the passengers were settled, the crew of the *Mayflower* began the long, hard journey back to England.

1. What is the main idea of the text? _____

_____

2. List at least two details that support the main idea.

_____

_____

3. What text structure did the author use? Underline the clues in the text that helped you decide.

_____

_____

4. What is the meaning of the phrase **the difficult task of settling in**?

_____

_____

Nonfiction Text Comprehension Prompts

Use the following cards to assess students' comprehension of nonfiction texts. You may choose to ask students the questions orally before, during, and after reading. Or, you can give students a card and ask them to respond in writing. Additionally, you may choose to use several cards to create an impromptu assessment for a text. Use cards A–E for before reading, cards F–K for during reading, and cards L–AD for after reading.

Look at the cover of the book and read the title. What do you think it is about? **A**	Look at the title of the text. What do you already know about this topic? What would you like to learn about this topic? **B**
Read the short summary on the back cover. What do you think this text is about? **C**	Skim through the text. What is one text feature the author used? Why would an author typically include that text feature? **D**
Analyze one text feature. What type is it? What did you learn by analyzing this feature? **E**	As you read, what are some words you did not know? What do you think they mean, based on the text? **F**

What is the main idea of the text?

What are some of the
supporting details?

G

What is the title of the text?

Is this a good one?

Why or why not?

H

What is the title of the text?

If you renamed the book, what
would you choose as the title?

Why?

I

What is one event from the text?

What caused this event to
happen?

J

What is one event from the text?

What happened because
of this event?

K

What is the purpose of this text?

Why did the author write it?

L

What are the five most important
words in the text?

Use those words
to write a summary.

M

Think about the text.

What are two things
you are wondering?

N

Create a time line that includes the most important events from the text.

O

Write a letter to the author that summarizes what you learned.

Close the letter with something new you would like to know.

P

What is one other text feature that the author could have included?

Create it on a separate sheet of paper.

Q

Compare and contrast two main topics in the text.

R

Think about the text.

What is one question you still have?

Where could you look to find the answer?

S

Create an acrostic poem about your topic.

T

What is the structure of the text?

How do you know?

U

What is the structure of the text?

Why do you think the author chose this structure?

V

What is one claim
the author makes?

How does the author
support this claim?

W

What is the author's
opinion about this topic?

Do you agree with the author?

Why or why not?

X

What is one problem
from the text?

How was it solved?

Y

List one connection
you have to the text.

How did this connection help
you better understand the text?

Z

Create a billboard to try to
convince your classmates
to read the text.

AA

If you were giving a grade
to the author, what grade
would you give him or her?

Why?

AB

What is your opinion
about the topic of this text?

Use evidence from the text to
support your thinking.

AC

What is the most interesting
thing you read in the text?

Why did it stand out to you?

AD

Making Inferences

Read. Then, answer the questions.

Where Is Amelia?

Amelia Earhart flew airplanes at a time when women rarely did such things. She made many daring trips and was the first woman to fly solo across the Atlantic Ocean. In 1937, Amelia planned to fly around the world. Instead, she **vanished** before completing her trip.

She and her copilot made it to the Pacific Ocean. On July 2, 1937, they planned to fly to a tiny island. However, many things went wrong. The day was supposed to be clear, but it was not. The flight took longer than planned. Amelia sent a message to say that her airplane was getting low on gas. In her last static-filled message, she said that she could not see the island. She was never heard from again.

The president of the United States called for a search. It lasted two weeks. No clues were ever found.

At first, people thought that the airplane had just run out of gas. It must have crashed into the sea and sunk too far to be found. Other people said that Earhart was looking for information about Japanese ships. Was Amelia Earhart a spy?

The search for Amelia Earhart still goes on. One person thought that he had found her grave. Other people have found parts of airplanes. They thought the parts were from the crash of Earhart's airplane. But, many airplanes crashed into the Pacific Ocean during World War II.

No proof has ever been found that Amelia Earhart was a spy. Her body and her airplane have never been found. We may never know the whole story about this great pilot. She is gone, but her story lives on.

1. What kind of woman do you think Amelia Earhart was?

_____

2. What evidence from the text supports this?

_____

_____

3. What is the meaning of the word **vanished**? How do you know?

_____

_____

4. What does the author mean by, "She is gone, but her story lives on."?

_____

_____

Reasons and Evidence

Read. Then, answer the questions.

Taking Care of Teeth

Long ago, people cleaned their teeth in many interesting ways. They scratched their teeth with sticks, wiped them with rags, or even chewed on crushed bones or shells. Luckily, tooth care has come a long way in the past few hundred years.

It took someone with a lot of time on his hands to invent the first mass-produced toothbrush. In the 1770s, a man named William Addis was in prison. He had an idea to make a tool for cleaning teeth. He used a bone and some bristles from a hairbrush. He carefully drilled holes in one end of the bone. Then, he trimmed the brush bristles and pushed them into the holes. He glued the bristles into place and had the first toothbrush.

People have used different tooth cleaners over the years. Many cleaners, such as crushed bones and shells, actually damaged the protective enamel on teeth. Chalk was a popular cleaner in the 1850s. Baking soda was also used for many years because it was abrasive. Other people used salt as a tooth cleaner. Some toothpastes still contain baking soda and sodium. Fluoride was first added to toothpaste in 1956. It greatly reduced the number of cavities in children. In the 1960s, calcium was added to toothpaste to help strengthen teeth.

Using dental floss once a day is one of the most important things that you can do for your teeth. Originally, floss was made of silk. Now, dental floss comes in different materials. Dental floss removes interproximal plaque accumulation, which means that it scrapes off the plaque that gathers between your teeth where a toothbrush cannot reach.

The inventions and improvements in dental care have helped people maintain stronger, healthier teeth. We now know how to better care for our teeth every day.

1. What is the author's opinion about how people used to clean their teeth?

_____

2. How does the author support this opinion?

_____

_____

3. How does the author support the idea that flossing once a day is one of the most important things you can do for your teeth?

_____

_____

4. What could be another title for this text?

_____

Text Structure

Read. Then, answer the questions.

Earthquakes

Ancient civilizations did not have scientific information to explain the causes of earthquakes. They made up stories that reveal their lack of understanding. Some of these ancient people believed that Earth was carried on the backs of animals.

Some Native Americans thought that a giant sea turtle held up Earth. They believed that when the turtle moved, Earth moved. When the turtle moved more, Earth moved more, causing cracks to form on Earth's surface.

In India, it was believed that four elephants held up Earth. They stood on the back of a turtle, and the turtle, in turn, balanced on the back of a snake. If any of these animals moved, Earth would shake and cause an earthquake. The greater the movement was, the greater the earthquake was.

The ancient Greeks thought that earthquakes showed the gods' anger. A giant, named Atlas, had **rebelled** against the gods, so he had to hold the world on his shoulders as punishment. The Greeks believed that any time Atlas adjusted Earth's weight on his shoulders, an earthquake would follow.

1. What is the main idea of this text?

_____

2. Compare and contrast the beliefs of Native Americans and Indians.

_____

_____

_____

3. What is the meaning of the word **rebelled**? How do you know?

_____

_____

4. What text structure did the author use?

_____

5. Why was this text structure the best to use?

_____

_____

Author's Purpose

Read. Then, answer the questions.

Rattlesnakes

Rattlesnakes are venomous reptiles whose home is anywhere from southern Canada in North America to Argentina in South America. There are 29 species of rattlesnakes. A large majority of them live in the southwestern United States and in Mexico.

A rattlesnake has excellent eyesight and a great sense of smell. Its forked tongue senses a combination of smells and tastes. It has ears but cannot receive outside sounds since an external and middle ear cavity are missing. It has an inner ear that enables it to detect ground vibrations.

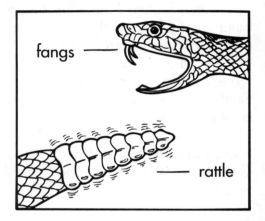

The rattlesnake has two long teeth called fangs. The fangs inject a bitten animal with the snake's venom. Rattlesnakes hunt and eat rodents, small birds, lizards, and frogs whole. Because snakes digest food slowly, a rattlesnake may not hunt again for several days.

The rattlesnake's rattle is probably its best known feature. It is a series of interlocking segments that vibrate whenever the tail shakes. When you hear its rattle, you do not want to go any closer.

1. How does the author describe a rattlesnake's tongue? _____

2. Why did the author include this comparison?

_____

3. Why did the author include the last sentence?

_____

4. Which text feature did the author include? _____

5. How did this text feature contribute to your understanding of the text?

_____

_____

6. How do you think detecting ground vibrations helps a rattlesnake?

_____

Understanding Main Idea

Read. Then, answer the questions.

The Brain

The brain is an organ of the body that controls almost everything the human body does. It has three main parts. Each part controls different bodily functions. The three parts are the medulla, the cerebellum, and the cerebrum.

The medulla is located where the spinal cord enters the head. It takes care of involuntary actions. Involuntary actions do not require any decision making. They happen without any thought. Breathing, digestion, and elimination are examples of involuntary actions.

Voluntary acts demand some instruction. Brushing one's teeth, dressing, or turning a somersault are examples of voluntary actions. The cerebellum is the part of the brain that controls bodily movement.

The largest part of the brain is the cerebrum. It controls voluntary mental operations such as the senses, muscles, speech, thinking, remembering, learning, and deciding. The cerebrum is divided into two equal parts called hemispheres. The hemispheres are covered by a layer of nerve cells called the cortex. There are many centers located in different areas of the cortex that send and receive messages. Each of the operations the cerebrum controls is located in a different center.

1. What is the main idea of paragraph two?

_____

2. What is the main idea of paragraph three?

_____

3. What is the main idea of paragraph four?

_____

4. Name one more thing the medulla would control.

_____

5. Name one more thing the cerebellum would control.

_____

6. Name one more thing the cerebrum would control.

_____

7. Which part of the brain would you use most at school? Why?

_____

Finding Text Evidence

Read. Then, answer the questions.

The Dewey Decimal System

Most school libraries look similar. Books are arranged in a certain way. Why is this important? It means you can find a book in a **precise** place. Books are organized by their subjects. If you know what the book is about, it is easy to find. Do you need a book on the environment? Look in the 300s. Do you want to look up facts on animals? The 500 section is the place to be. Do you need a cookbook? Skip over to the 600s. You can find the books you need if you know a few rules.

Books were not always organized this way. Each library arranged books differently. One library might order books by purchase date. Another library might have all the green books together. Another could alphabetize all of the books by title. This must have been very confusing for visitors.

In the late 1800s, Melvil Dewey was a librarian. He wanted to reorganize libraries. He wanted to organize them all the same way. Mr. Dewey came up with 10 major divisions for books. Each major division is also divided into sections. The 10 major divisions are listed below:

000 – General works		500 – Sciences	
100 – Psychology		600 – Technology	
200 – Religion		700 – Arts and Recreation	
300 – Social Sciences		800 – Literature	
400 – Language		900 – Geography and History	

This is how most school libraries are set up. Mr. Dewey's work means you can find the same book in the same place in most libraries.

1. What is the meaning of the word **precise**? Use text evidence to support your answer.

_____

_____

2. How did the author organize the first paragraph?

_____

3. What is the main idea of this text?

_____

_____

4. Where would you find a book on computers? _____

5. Create a book title you might find in the 500s.

_____

Informational Text Comprehension

Read. Then, answer the questions.

The Gravity of Childhood

Sir Isaac Newton was the first person to be able to explain gravity. He was a very important scientist and thinker. But, his life had a rough start. He was born in 1642. His father had just died. His mother married again. Her new husband did not want Isaac. So, the little boy was raised by his grandmother.

When Isaac started school, he was ranked second from the last in his grade! But, he was a good student. He spent much of his time outside. He flew kites and watched how the wind moved them. He **observed** the clouds and the stars. He was always busy and always thinking.

The hard work paid off. When he left school, he was first in his class. All of the time he spent watching the natural world paid off too. One day, he looked out a window and saw an apple fall from a tree. He wondered why apples always fall to the ground. Why do they not ever fall up or sideways?

That was when Isaac first started thinking about gravity, the force that pulls things toward Earth. It was only one of his important ideas. He also wrote about color and light. Isaac Newton thought of many of his famous ideas during his lonely but thoughtful childhood.

1. What is the meaning of the word **observed**?

_____

2. How did the author organize the text?

_____

3. What is the main idea?

_____

_____

4. How does the author support the statement, "But, his life had a rough start."?

_____

_____

5. Why do you think Isaac came up with so many important ideas?

_____

_____

Key Details

Read. Then, answer the questions.

Northern Lights

You may see them in the north in the nighttime sky. They begin with a **slight** shimmer in the sky. Within minutes, thin poles of light ripple across the sky. The lights are greenish or white in the center and slightly violet or red at the edges. They flow like a blanket being shaken out at the beach. They are known as the northern lights, or aurora borealis. They will take your breath away for 10 to 20 minutes, then fade away.

The aurora borealis starts on our nearest star, the sun. On the sun, extremely hot gas particles are very excited. They create a state of matter called plasma. This plasma escapes the sun's corona, or atmosphere. These particles, called a solar wind, spray out like water from a hose that someone swings in a circle over his head. The solar wind travels through space. If it is aimed at Earth, it is attracted to Earth's magnetic field surrounding the north and south poles.

When this solar wind hits Earth's atmosphere, the particles strike atoms. These atoms release a burst of color. The storm of particles hitting the atmosphere is called an aurora substorm. When the plasma particles stop striking, the brilliant light show known as the aurora borealis stops.

1. What is the meaning of the word **slight**? _____

_____

2. What would be another good title for this text? Why? _____

_____

3. What is the solar wind attracted to? _____

_____

4. What is the main idea of the text? _____

_____

5. List details that support the main idea. _____

_____

A

Main Idea

Supporting Detail	Supporting Detail

B

Title _____

_____

Text Structure _____

_____

I know this because _____

_____ .

C

Title _____

_____

Two things I learned _____

_____

One thing I still want to know_____

_____

D

Title _____

Summary _____

_____

_____

Did you like this book? Why or why not?

_____

E

New word _____

_____

Definition _____

_____

In a sentence _____

_____

F

Title _____

_____

Inference _____

_____

Evidence _____

_____

G

Title _____

Text Feature _____

_____

How did it help you understand the text?

_____

_____

H

Create another text feature for the text.

Create a topic web for the text.

I

Create a time line of the subject's life.

J

Create a diagram to support the text.

K

Is this a firsthand or secondhand account?

_____

How do you know?

_____
_____
_____

L

How would this text be different if it were a secondhand account? _____

_____
_____
_____
_____

M

Name one opinion from the text.

_____
_____

How does the author support this opinion?

_____
_____

N

Whoa! I was very interested by:

_____
_____
_____
_____

O

Write one thing you are clear about and one thing that confuses you.

P

Word Lists

Use these lists of words when you are assessing spelling and decoding concepts. The lists are not comprehensive but can be used as grade-level examples for creating your own assessments, flash cards, etc.

Long-Vowel Patterns

bone
chain
flute
kite
mule
peach
queen
smoke
soap
stove
teeth
toad

R-Controlled Vowels

sharp
barb
stern
clerk
thirst
twirl
storm
scorn
nurse
curb
warn
march

Diphthongs

auction
couch
drawn
enjoy
frown
gloom
groom
royal
spoil
stalk
stood
taught
voice

Consonant Clusters

bridge
catch
gnat
knowledge
scratch
shrank
sponge
spread
squeeze
straight
thrill
wrinkle

Contractions

could've
couldn't
doesn't
here's
might've
they'll
weren't
where's
who'll
who's
would've
you'll

Inflectional Endings (-s/-es/-ed)

plants
houses
boxes
dishes
inches
snowed
screamed
started
needed
walked
asked
picked

Word Lists

Inflectional Endings (*-ing*)

asking
cleaning
closing
dreaming
moving
picking
reading
running
skating
stopping
swimming
taking

Compound Words

anything
beside
bookmark
checkout
downstairs
everyone
flashlight
headphones
myself
snowman
somewhere
throughout

Accented Syllables

always
arrive
caution
excuse
forty
learner
loyal
people
perfect
remain
remote
thousand

Unaccented Syllables

begun
couple
doctor
dollar
evil
napkin
nature
pleasure
spider
stolen
teacher
total

Affixes

(See page 70 for lists of words with affixes.)

Consonants (Hard and Soft *c/g*)

cereal
cent
practice
decimal
receive
topic
common
camera
gentle
giraffe
angel
garage
garbage
sugar
giggle
angle

Consonants (Final /k/ Sounds)

gigantic
magnetic
republic
topic
click
shock
stuck
trick
daybreak
soak
squeak
week
awake
hike
mistake
hike

The Mysterious Light

Jan sat in a chair by the window. The grandfather clock at the bottom of the stairs started to chime and it echoed through the quiet farmhouse. Jan could barely keep her eyes open. She knew her pajamas were folded neatly on the bed, but she didn't want to wear them. If she had to run for help, she wanted to be in her jeans, a shirt, and tennis shoes.

When her mom and dad explained that she could visit her aunt and uncle while her parents were visiting France, she was excited. Her other choice was Camp Rainbow and she hated it there. At least at the farm she would have her own room, excellent food, and no leather crafts.

She closed her eyes and counted the clock's strikes—9, 10, 11, 12. She now wished she had selected Camp Rainbow. It wasn't perfect but it was better than a spooky, old farmhouse. The clock stopped chiming, and the house was silent. Jan opened her eyes and looked down on the garden. She wanted to see the mysterious light again. If she knew what it was, she might be able to sleep.

At first, she saw nothing but dark paths and the reflection of the half moon on the pond. Maybe the light that she saw the night before was just her imagination. Suddenly, she saw it again. The light beam flickered, and then it was steady. When it moved toward the farmhouse, Jan dove into bed. Her heart pounded as her bedroom door slowly creaked open. She tried to stay perfectly still, but she couldn't help shaking when a voice called her name. "Jan, are you still awake?"

She sat up in bed and questioned, "Uncle Jason, is that you?"

"Yes. I was outside checking on the barn and noticed that Rose had her kittens. Would you like to come visit them?"

"Sure!" said Jan. She hopped out of bed and reached for her shoes.

Her uncle looked puzzled. "Jan, why are you wearing your clothes in bed?"

Jan laughed. "It's a long story, Uncle Jason. I'll tell you on the way to the barn."

The Mysterious Light

Jan sat in a chair by the window. The grandfather clock at the bottom of the stairs   17
started to chime and it echoed through the quiet farmhouse. Jan could barely keep her   32
eyes open. She knew her pajamas were folded neatly on the bed, but she didn't want to   49
wear them. If she had to run for help, she wanted to be in her jeans, a shirt, and tennis   69
shoes.   70

When her mom and dad explained that she could visit her aunt and uncle while   85
her parents were visiting France, she was excited. Her other choice was Camp Rainbow   99
and she hated it there. At least at the farm she would have her own room, excellent   116
food, and no leather crafts.   121

She closed her eyes and counted the clock's strikes—9, 10, 11, 12. She now   136
wished she had selected Camp Rainbow. It wasn't perfect but it was better than a   151
spooky, old farmhouse. The clock stopped chiming, and the house was silent. Jan   164
opened her eyes and looked down on the garden. She wanted to see the mysterious   179
light again. If she knew what it was, she might be able to sleep.   193

At first, she saw nothing but dark paths and the reflection of the half moon on the   210
pond. Maybe the light that she saw the night before was just her imagination. Suddenly   225
she saw it again. The light beam flickered, and then it was steady. When it moved   241
toward the farmhouse, Jan dove into bed. Her heart pounded as her bedroom door   255
slowly creaked open. She tried to stay perfectly still, but she couldn't help shaking when   270
a voice called her name. "Jan, are you still awake?"   280

She sat up in bed and questioned, "Uncle Jason, is that you?"   292

"Yes. I was outside checking on the barn and noticed that Rose had her kittens.   307
Would you like to come visit them?"   314

"Sure!" said Jan. She hopped out of bed and reached for her shoes.   327

Her uncle looked puzzled. "Jan, why are you wearing your clothes in bed?"   340

Jan laughed. "It's a long story, Uncle Jason. I'll tell you on the way to the barn."   357

Number of Words Read	Words per Minute	Words Read in Error
First Try		
Second Try		
Third Try		

A Family Hike

We started on the trail early in the morning. The sun was rising in the sky and the air around us was cool and misty. The pine needles looked like arrows pointing our way to the top of the mountain.

My mom and dad each carried a heavy backpack filled with food, tents, water, and other things. Pablo and I carried backpacks also. Mine only had my clothes and a sleeping bag inside. I carried a few snacks in my pockets and two water bottles on my belt. Pablo carried some food and a cookstove in his pack.

We walked quietly at first. My dad says you don't need words to be part of the forest in the morning. I could hear birds singing and chipmunks moving through the leaves on the ground. There was no breeze, so the trees were silent.

At lunchtime, we stopped by a stream that flowed down the mountain. We could see a small waterfall higher up, but here the water cut through the rock and snaked past flowers and bushes. We took off our shoes and dipped our feet in the water. The sun shone brightly overhead, and we all took off our jackets.

I knew better than to ask how much farther we had to go. We would be walking for three more days on these trails, and we would see many beautiful sights and hear and smell things we don't hear or smell at home in the city. My mom and dad are teachers, and every summer we take a trip as a family.

We went to bed pretty early because we were all tired from walking. We will reach the top of the mountain tomorrow. My dad says that I will be able to see forever, and I think I'll like that. But, that is tomorrow, and my dad says that even the night is part of the journey. So, I will close my eyes and listen for the owls, the wind in the trees, and the sound of my dad snoring. I love this place!

A Family Hike

We started on the trail early in the morning. The sun was rising in the sky and the   18
air around us was cool and misty. The pine needles looked like arrows pointing our way   34
to the top of the mountain.   40

My mom and dad each carried a heavy backpack filled with food, tents, water,   54
and other things. Pablo and I carried backpacks also. Mine only had my clothes and a   70
sleeping bag inside. I carried a few snacks in my pockets and two water bottles on my   87
belt. Pablo carried some food and a cookstove in his pack.   98

We walked quietly at first. My dad says you don't need words to be part of the   115
forest in the morning. I could hear birds singing and chipmunks moving through the   129
leaves on the ground. There was no breeze, so the trees were silent.   142

At lunchtime, we stopped by a stream that flowed down the mountain. We could   156
see a small waterfall higher up, but here the water cut through the rock and snaked past   173
flowers and bushes. We took off our shoes, and dipped our feet in the water. The sun   190
shone brightly overhead, and we all took off our jackets.   200

I knew better than to ask how much farther we had to go. We would be walking for   218
three more days on these trails, and we would see many beautiful sights and hear and   234
smell things we don't hear or smell at home in the city. My mom and dad are teachers,   252
and every summer we take a trip as a family.   262

We went to bed pretty early because we were all tired from walking. We will reach   278
the top of the mountain tomorrow. My dad says that I will be able to see forever, and I   297
think I'll like that. But, that is tomorrow, and my dad says that even the night is part of   316
the journey. So, I will close my eyes and listen for the owls, the wind in the trees, and the   336
sound of my dad snoring. I love this place!   345

Number of Words Read	Words per Minute	Words Read in Error
First Try		
Second Try		
Third Try		

Insects in Winter

In the summertime, insects can be seen buzzing and fluttering around us. But, as winter's cold weather begins, the insects seem to disappear. Do you know where they go? Many insects find a warm place to spend the winter.

Ants try to dig deep into the ground. Some beetles stack up in piles under rocks or dead leaves. Certain butterflies take a trip south for the season. Ladybugs may find a quiet hiding spot inside the attic of a house. Spiders, although not truly insects, might crawl into pockets of leaves and grass that are underneath the snow.

Female grasshoppers don't even stay around for winter. In autumn, they lay their eggs and then die. The eggs hatch in the spring.

Bees also try to protect themselves from the frigid winter. Honeybees gather into a ball in the middle of their hive. The bees stay in this tight ball trying to stay warm.

Dragonflies in their second stage of life winter under water. They stay active as they are growing and find food beneath the surface. This keeps them from freezing.

Woolly bear caterpillars actually allow parts of their bodies to freeze. This protects them by preventing the entire body from freezing. They stay in this state until warmer weather arrives.

Winter is very hard for insects, but each spring the survivors come out, and the buzzing and fluttering begin again.

Insects in Winter

In the summertime, insects can be seen buzzing and fluttering around us. But, as 14
winter's cold weather begins, the insects seem to disappear. Do you know where they 28
go? Many insects find a warm place to spend the winter. 39

Ants try to dig deep into the ground. Some beetles stack up in piles under rocks 55
or dead leaves. Certain butterflies take a trip south for the season. Ladybugs may find 70
a quiet hiding spot inside the attic of a house. Spiders, although not truly insects, might 86
crawl into pockets of leaves and grass that are underneath the snow. 98

Female grasshoppers don't even stay around for winter. In autumn, they lay their 111
eggs and then die. The eggs hatch in the spring. 121

Bees also try to protect themselves from the frigid winter. Honeybees gather into a 135
ball in the middle of their hive. The bees stay in this tight ball trying to stay warm. 153

Dragonflies in their second stage of life winter under water. They stay active as they 168
are growing and find food beneath the surface. This keeps them from freezing. 181

Woolly bear caterpillars actually allow parts of their bodies to freeze. This protects 194
them by preventing the entire body from freezing. They stay in this state until warmer 209
weather arrives. 211

Winter is very hard for insects, but each spring the survivors come out, and the 226
buzzing and fluttering begin again. 231

Number of Words Read	Words per Minute	Words Read in Error
First Try		
Second Try		
Third Try		

Wolves

If you have read fairy tales, you may believe that all wolves are mean, evil, and ruthless. They eat children, pigs, and other small animals. There is not anything good to say about wolves. Or, is there?

Wolves are actually nothing like the characters in fairy tales. While they do eat animals, wolves would never attack a person just for the sake of eating them. They may attack people if the people threaten them. This happens rarely. Wolves tend to be shy animals.

Wolves are meat eaters and they must hunt to get their food. They are strong and fast and have sharp teeth. They use their sense of smell to find prey. They usually hunt the weakest, slowest animal in a group. Wolves are not cruel; they are just good hunters.

Some wolves are near extinction. Their homes are disappearing as people move further into the wilderness. Wolves have also been hunted.

Ranchers and farmers pose another threat to wolves. They become angry when wolves eat their chickens and sheep. This is a serious problem, because the farmers lose their animals and the wolves are shot by the angry farmers. No one wins in this battle.

Wolves are an important part of the balance of nature. They hunt weak animals and keep down the populations. In many countries, it is now against the law to hunt wolves. Many zoos and scientists are working hard to protect wolves because they understand just how important wolves really are.

Wolves

If you have read fairy tales, you may believe that all wolves are mean, evil, and	16
ruthless. They eat children, pigs, and other small animals. There is not anything good to	31
say about wolves. Or, is there?	37
Wolves are actually nothing like the characters in fairy tales. While they do eat	51
animals, wolves would never attack a person just for the sake of eating them. They may	67
attack people if the people threaten them. This happens rarely. Wolves tend to be shy	82
animals.	83
Wolves are meat eaters and they must hunt to get their food. They are strong and	98
fast and have sharp teeth. They use their sense of smell to find prey. They usually hunt	115
the weakest, slowest animal in a group. Wolves are not cruel; they are just good	131
hunters.	132
Some wolves are near extinction. Their homes are disappearing as people move	144
further into the wilderness. Wolves have also been hunted.	153
Ranchers and farmers pose another threat to wolves. They become angry when	165
wolves eat their chickens and sheep. This is a serious problem, because the farmers lose	180
their animals and the wolves are shot by the angry farmers. No one wins in this battle.	197
Wolves are an important part of the balance of nature. They hunt weak animals	211
and keep down the populations. In many countries, it is now against the law to hunt	227
wolves. Many zoos and scientists are working hard to protect wolves because they	240
understand just how important wolves really are.	247

Number of Words Read	Words per Minute	Words Read in Error
First Try		
Second Try		
Third Try		

The Miller's Daughter (excerpt)

Alfred, Lord Tennyson

I see the wealthy miller yet,
His double chin, his portly size,
And who that knew him could forget
The busy wrinkles round his eyes?
The slow wise smile that, round about
His dusty forehead drily curl'd,
Seem'd half-within and half-without,
And full of dealings with the world?

In yonder chair I see him sit,
Three fingers round the old silver cup
I see his gray eyes twinkle yet
At his own jest gray eyes lit up
With summer lightnings of a soul
So full of summer warmth, so glad,
So healthy, sound, and clear and whole,
His memory scarce can make me sad.

The Miller's Daughter (excerpt)

Alfred, Lord Tennyson

I see the wealthy miller yet,	6
His double chin, his portly size,	12
And who that knew him could forget	19
The busy wrinkles round his eyes?	25
The slow wise smile that, round about	32
His dusty forehead drily curl'd,	37
Seem'd half-within and half-without,	41
And full of dealings with the world?	48
In yonder chair I see him sit,	55
Three fingers round the old silver cup	62
I see his gray eyes twinkle yet	69
At his own jest gray eyes lit up	77
With summer lightnings of a soul	83
So full of summer warmth, so glad,	90
So healthy, sound, and clear and whole,	97
His memory scarce can make me sad.	104

Number of Words Read	Words per Minute	Words Read in Error
First Try		
Second Try		
Third Try		

Comprehension Questions

The Mysterious Light (pages 43 and 44)
1. Where is Jan?
2. Where are Jan's parents?
3. What caused the mysterious light?
4. Why did Jan wear her clothes to bed?

A Family Hike (pages 45 and 46)
1. Where is the family?
2. Name some things they see on their hike.
3. What do Mom and Dad do for a living?
4. When does the family travel?

Insects in Winter (pages 47 and 48)
1. What do ants do in the winter?
2. How do bees stay warm?
3. What makes winter hard for insects?
4. Which insect might sleep in your house?

Wolves (pages 49 and 50)
1. What type of animal are wolves?
2. What do wolves eat?
3. Why are wolves in danger?
4. Why are wolves important?

The Miller's Daughter (pages 51 and 52)
1. Describe the miller.
2. Where is the miller?
3. What is the miller holding?
4. What season is it?

Today I read _____ words per minute.

At this point I should be reading _____ words per minute.

My goal is to read _____ words per minute on my next timed reading.

A

Today I read _____ words per minute.

I read _____ words incorrectly.

My accuracy percentage is _____ %.

At this point I should be reading with _____ % accuracy.

My goal is to have _____ % accuracy.

B

List each word you had trouble reading today and the strategy you used to decode it.

C

Find two multisyllabic words from the text. List them below, along with their definition.

D

Find three words from the text with an affix. Complete the chart below.

Prefix	Base	Suffix

E

List one word from the text for which you did not know the meaning. Which context clues helped you figure out the meaning?

_____

_____

_____

_____

F

Assess your oral reading skills.

	Yes	No
I changed my tone of voice to reflect the mood.		
I used different voices to reflect the characters.		
I read with good speed and volume.		

G

List one reading goal.

_____

_____

How do you plan to meet this goal?

_____

_____

H

The following cards contain writing prompts. Use one for a whole-class writing assessment, or laminate them and place them in a writing center. Cards A–G are opinion prompts, cards H–P are informative/explanative prompts, cards Q–Z are narrative/descriptive prompts, and cards AA–AD are research prompts.

There are many things at school that adults and students do not always agree about. Think about one thing at school you would like to change. Write a letter to your teacher about this topic.

A

The fourth-grade teachers want to plan a field trip to somewhere fun. The principal requires that the trip be educational and related to the curriculum. Write a letter to the principal about your choice.

B

Think about a recent book you have read. Write a review of the book.

C

Create a report card for your teacher. Include grades and comments about at least five topics.

D

Write a paragraph explaining which chores you should complete at home and why.

E

Think of one issue facing kids today. Write a letter to the president about your opinion on this issue.

F

Write a paper about what you think should happen to students who misbehave at school.

G

Think about something that you do well. Create a presentation that clearly explains this topic.

H

Think about the current science unit. Create a booklet that the class could use to review.

I

Write a paper explaining how to play your favorite game.

J

Write a schedule of your day. Include a description of each time period.

K

Think about a living creature that has adapted to survive. Write about how and why it has adapted.

L

Write about your favorite holiday experience.

M

Describe the differences between wild animals and pets.

N

Pick one person that you know and admire. Write a biography about his or her life. Include a time line and illustration.

O

Write a letter to your best friend explaining why you think he or she is wonderful.

P

Imagine a perfect day with your family. Describe it.

Q

Find an interesting photograph. Write a story that could go with the photo.

R

Imagine you've found a magic pebble. How did you find it and what happens once you pick it up?

S

Imagine waking up in another country. Write about where you are and what happens.

T

On the way home you meet a talking animal. Which kind of animal is it and what happens once it begins talking?

U

You've been granted magical powers. What will you do?

V

On the way to the park you find one million dollars. What will you do?

W

Think about the plot of a story you have recently read.

Complete an acrostic poem using the main character's name.

X

Think about a problem in your life. Write about an invention that solves that problem.

Y

Imagine life without television. Write what it would be like.

Z

Research your favorite animal. Create a poster about the animal.

AA

Complete research about your state flag. Write a paper explaining its history.

AB

Investigate an important time period in history. Write a paper about this time period.

AC

Research your favorite president or historical figure.

Write a biography about his or her life.

AD

Editing Writing

Read the paragraph. Circle the errors. Rewrite the paragraph and correct each mistake.

Last week I go to my aunts house. It was my cousin's birthday and they were haveing a party to celebrate. she was turning for and wanted a princess party i was asked to be the prince. At first. I didnt want too do it but then my Uncle called me and offerd to take me to a basketball game if I did. when I arrived. my cousin ran up and jumped in my arms. Most of her freinds were already their. Aunt heather had gotten a crown and a purple robe for me to where. I quickly dressed and join the girls in the backyard. I helped them paint there nails and then create their own crownes. After Jessica opened her gifts it was time for cake. She had picked out a pink, square won with purple flowers on top. After everyone left, Jessica crawled into my lap and hugged me. She was so tired, she fell asleep. After I laid her down i drive home. The party wasnt nearly as bad as I thought it would be.

_____
_____
_____
_____
_____
_____
_____
_____
_____
_____
_____
_____
_____
_____
_____
_____

Name _____ Date _____

Editing and Revising Writing

Read the paragraph. Circle the errors. Rewrite the paragraph and correct each mistake. Be sure to correct errors in organization and improve word choice.

    Carter and Nick have ben freinds for their lives. They live next dore to each other and are in same class at school. Both boys have to younger sisters and one older brother they even play on the same baseball team. When they meat someone new they like to pretend they are twins? There parents let them every afternoon do homework together every afternoon. As soon as they finish, they run outside and play until it is time for breakfast. Fortunately, carter just found out he is moveing away. Got a new job in another state. There parents have talking and decided that the boys can visit each other every summer four two weeks. They have also set up email accounts and can right each other every day. They no it wont be the same, but they plan to remain friends forever!

_____

_____

_____

_____

_____

_____

_____

_____

_____

_____

_____

_____

_____

_____

_____

_____

How did you organize your writing?

_____

Why did you organize it this way?

_____

_____

_____

A

Write one opinion about today's lesson.

_____

List at least three details to support your opinion.

_____

_____

_____

B

List linking/transition words and phrases that will help when writing an opinion piece.

_____

_____

_____

_____

C

Who read your writing today?

_____

What suggestions did he or she give you?

_____

_____

_____

D

What did you focus on today?

editing   revising

What types of mistakes did you find?

_____

_____

_____

E

Which text feature did you include in your writing?

_____

How will this help the reader better understand the topic?

_____

_____

_____

F

List linking/transition words and phrases that will help when writing an informative piece.

_____

_____

_____

_____

G

List the number of each type of sentence in your writing.

_____ declarative

_____ interrogative

_____ exclamatory

Revise your writing based on what you found.

H

Which topic are you writing about?

_____

What words will be important to include?

_____

_____

_____

I

List linking/transitional words and phrases that will help you when writing a narrative.

_____

_____

_____

_____

J

List one example of figurative language that you used in your writing.

_____

Why did you choose to include it?

_____

_____

K

List one sentence from your story.

_____

Add at least two more descriptive words that show rather than tell. Rewrite the sentence.

_____

_____

L

Create a list of items you should consider when revising a piece of writing.

_____

_____

_____

_____

M

Create a list of items you should consider when editing a piece of writing.

_____

_____

_____

_____

N

List three websites you visited to complete your research today.

_____

_____

_____

_____

O

Write the opinion or point the author is trying to make.

_____

_____

How did the author support this opinion or point?

_____

_____

P

✦ Show What You Know ✦
Grammar and Usage

Look at each underlined word. Write a word from the word bank that tells what part of speech it is.

conjunction	modal verb	preposition	pronoun

_____ **1.** I don't know <u>which</u> of you is right.

_____ **2.** Mrs. Sabatino told the class to put our notes <u>inside</u> our desks.

_____ **3.** Noah's mother said he <u>could</u> play outside after lunch.

Circle the progressive verbs in each sentence.

4. My mom is baking my birthday cake.

5. Molly will be studying hard all night long.

Read the sentences. Circle the word that best completes each sentence.

6. Marisa asked her father if she could (by, buy) a new backpack.

7. Elijah couldn't (hear, here) his mother because his music was too loud.

8. The team was excited when they (won, one) their first game.

Write **S** for sentence, **F** for fragment, and **R** for run-on.

_____ **9.** Javon wanted to play soccer.

_____ **10.** Won the game last weekend

_____ **11.** I play baseball my team won the game.

Circle the relative adverb in each sentence.

12. Mrs. Benson asked me where I was going after school.

13. Paul told his mom why he was late getting home.

Circle the relative pronoun in each sentence.

14. Philip asked who was going to the concert next weekend.

15. Do you know whose backpack this is?

Change the sentence to show the progressive verb tense.

16. She sighed at her pesky brother. _____

✦ Show What You Know ✦
Grammar and Usage

Look at each underlined word. Write a word from the word bank that tells what part of speech it is.

conjunction	modal verb	preposition	pronoun

_____ **1.** I threw the ball <u>across</u> the field.

_____ **2.** Ivy wanted to know <u>who</u> would help her clean the kitchen.

_____ **3.** Parker <u>quickly</u> did his homework so that he could watch TV.

Circle the progressive verbs in each sentence.

4. The fans were cheering loudly for the home team.

5. I am going to spend the night at my aunt's house.

Read the sentences. Circle the word that best completes each sentence.

6. (Its, It's) going to take a long time to play that game.

7. Malia asked her mother (four, for) a ride to the library.

8. Megan asked me if I (knew, new) about her (knew, new) phone.

Write **S** for sentence, **F** for fragment, and **R** for run-on.

_____ **9.** Dylan worked hard his mom gave him a treat.

_____ **10.** Cody studied harder for the test than anyone in our class.

_____ **11.** Floating in the pool!

Circle the relative adverb in each sentence.

12. Before I left, Mom told me when I needed to be home.

13. I asked my teacher where I should turn in my homework.

Circle the relative pronoun in each sentence.

14. Dad said I could take whomever I wanted to the movies with us.

15. Do you know which lunchbox is Seth's?

Change the sentence to show the progressive verb tense.

16. I jumped rope with my friend. _____

✦ Show What You Know ✦
Conventions

Write **C** for correct and **I** for incorrect.

_____ **1.** "Mom asked Susan, Can you hand me that book?"

_____ **2.** "I would like to go to the movies", said David.

_____ **3.** Mrs. Smith said, "Please take out your science books."

_____ **4.** "Let's go to the pool" suggested Susan.

_____ **5.** I need to do my laundry but, we have no soap or softener.

_____ **6.** Jordan asked for a pencil, and then she did her classwork.

_____ **7.** Mom got off of work later than usual so she, picked up a pizza on the way home.

Add the correct punctuation to each sentence.

8. Do you want spaghetti for dinner asked Dad

9. I can't believe we won $1,000 screamed Byron

10. Please clean your room requested mom Then you can play games

11. I know you want to watch TV but first you must finish your chores

12. Last night's snow broke all previous records and school will be closed for days because of the storm

13. Jawan moved to Austin Texas from Los Angeles California

14. Mr. Lee said Please clear your desks and take out two pencils

15. I can't wait to go to middle school exclaimed Myong It is going to be so much fun

Read the paragraph. Circle each error.

Last weekend my parents take us to new york city. We had such a grate time? i got too visit a toy store and my dad bought us for new game. We road in a yellow cab mom wanted to visit the zoo. Their were a bunch of knew baby elephants. They were so cute! After the zoo we ate hot dogs at a food cart but then we took the subway. I cant imagine having more fun any where. When my parents ask me where we should go next, I told them orlando florida. I here theres a mouse there I can meat!

✦ Show What You Know
Conventions

Write **C** for correct and **I** for incorrect.

_____ **1.** Dad asked Brock, "Would you like pizza for dinner?"

_____ **2.** Jim answered ",I have very little homework."

_____ **3.** "I really want to go to the beach exclaimed Kim!"

_____ **4.** "Let's study for the test after school," suggested Dave.

_____ **5.** Dad stopped by the store after work but he forgot to get the sunblock.

_____ **6.** Tom cleaned his bedroom and bathroom, and Maria cleaned the kitchen and did the laundry.

_____ **7.** Adam couldn't make up his mind so, he asked his best friend for advice.

Add the correct punctuation to each sentence.

8. Libby is coming over after dinner said Mom

9. That was the best roller coaster ever exclaimed Owen

10. We need to take our test stated Mrs. Foster Then we can have recess

11. We spent all morning going from one garage sale to the next and then my mom took me out to lunch at my favorite restaurant

12. I wanted to study for our spelling test at Paige's house but my mom made me stay home and work on my math homework with Dad

13. My mom got a new job so we will be moving from Detroit Michigan to Atlanta Georgia

14. Mr. Martinez asked Would you like to take the attendance to the office

15. Our team won the semi-final game explained Luke That means we are in the championship game

Read the paragraph. Circle each error.

Macon Silva lives in dallas texas. His younger sister is too years old she follows him everywhere he gose. Most kids would find that annoying. Not macon. He adores his little sister! he was twelve years old when she is born. He wished for a brother but his mom always said If wishes were horses, dreamers would ride. He wasnt sure what that meant, but he new he didnt care. Olivia giggles at everything and is allot of fun! Macon cant wait to watch her grow up.

Name _____ Date _____

✦ Show What You Know ✦
Word Meanings

Use context clues to circle the word that best matches the meaning of the underlined word.

1. My mom was <u>enraged</u> when she found out I broke her favorite mug.

    excited   hopeful   angry   depressed

2. Do not remain friends with someone who <u>deserts</u> you at the first sign of trouble.

    picks   carries   leaves   helps

3. The sound of thunder <u>startled</u> the baby.

    angered   scared   pleased   excited

Look at the following words. Circle the prefixes, underline the root words, and box the suffixes.

4. incredible   **5.** subtraction   **6.** repayment

7. bicycle   **8.** construction   **9.** biography

Answer each question.

10. If **active** means energy, what does **hyperactive** mean?

_____

11. If **lead** means to be in charge, what does **mislead** mean?

_____

12. If **stop** means to come to an end, what does **nonstop** mean?

_____

Write an antonym and a synonym for each word below.

	Antonym	**Synonym**
13. happy		
14. friendly		
15. beautiful		
16. large		

✦ Show What You Know ✦
Word Meanings

Use context clues to circle the word that best matches the meaning of the underlined word.

1. My dad was <u>ecstatic</u> when our team won the championship.

      excited   hopeful   angry   depressed

2. It is dangerous to eat anything that is <u>toxic</u>.

      spoiled   harmless   harmful   delicious

3. Kennedy is very <u>charming</u> and makes friends easily.

      different   loud   happy   pleasant

Look at the following words. Circle the prefixes, underline the root words, and box the suffixes.

4. hyperactive   **5.** autobiography   **6.** destruction

7. mistaken   **8.** encouragement   **9.** telephone

Answer each question.

10. If **scope** means to look or view, what does **microscope** mean?

_____

11. If **heat** means to warm something, what does **reheat** mean?

_____

12. If **aware** means to be alert, what does **unaware** mean?

_____

Write an antonym and a synonym for each word below.

	Antonym	**Synonym**
13. angry		
14. tall		
15. sad		
16. cold		

Word Lists

Use these lists of words when you are assessing language concepts. The lists are not comprehensive but can be used as grade-level examples for creating your own assessments, flash cards, etc.

Relative Pronouns
that
which
whichever
who
whoever
whom
whomever
whose

Relative Adverbs
when
where
why

Modal Verbs
can
could
may
might
must
ought
shall
should
will
would

Coordinating Conjunctions
and
but
for
nor
or
so
yet

Present Progressive Verbs
is baking
is driving
is eating
is jumping
is shopping
is studying
is talking
is walking
is waving
is writing

Past Progressive Verbs
was/were baking
was/were driving
was/were eating
was/were jumping
was/were shopping
was/were studying
was/were talking
was/were walking
was/were waving
was/were writing

Future Progressive Verbs
will be baking
will be driving
will be eating
will be jumping
will be shopping
will be studying
will be talking
will be walking
will be waving
will be writing

Word Lists

Words with Affixes and Roots

audience
autograph
automobile
bankrupt
biography
biology
century
chronological
colonial
conduct
construction
defeat
disruptive
fraction
homonym
hyperactive
inspect
microscope
midfield
misbehave
multiple
nonsense
overhead
prejudice
prescribe
quadrilateral
rejection
section
speedometer
telegram
telephone
television
thermometer
tighten
unusual

Homophones

aunt/ant
bare/bear
be/bee
blew/blue
brake/break*
by/buy*
cent/scent
clothes/close
dear/deer
eight/ate
flower/flour
grate/great
grown/groan
hear/here*
hour/our
I/eye
its/it's*
knew/new
knight/night
made/maid
male/mail
meat/meet*
oar/or
one/won
pair/pear
passed/past
peace/piece
plane/plain
poor/pour
pray/prey
right/write*
see/sea
sell/cell
so/sew/sow
some/sum
son/sun
they're/their/there*
to/two/too*
waste/waist
weak/week*
weigh/way
whole/hole
whose/who's*
your/you're*

Homographs

address
ball
bass
bat
bow
break
can
cool
desert
dove
drop
fair
fall
light
match
minute
object
park
pen
play
present
read
right
ring
rock
roll
rose
row
ship
sink
spring
tear
train
trip
trunk
wave
wind

*Frequently confused words

Relative Pronouns

Underline the relative pronoun in each sentence. Then, circle the clause it introduces.

1. Which of you is having a birthday in May?

2. The team who won the tournament is happy.

3. This is the book that I read.

4. He is the kind of teacher that everyone likes.

5. My mom told me I could invite whomever I wanted to the party.

6. Here are the hot dogs that my father made for dinner.

7. You can choose whichever cookie you want for dessert.

8. Can you tell me whose backpack this is?

9. Whose paper is that on the floor?

10. Whoever wins the spelling bee will advance on to the district level.

Write a sentence using each relative pronoun below. Circle the noun that it identifies.

11. who

_____

12. whose

_____

13. which

_____

14. that

_____

15. whoever

_____

Adverbs

Circle the adverb in each sentence.

1. She quickly finished her homework so that she could play outside.

2. My dad often drinks coffee in the morning.

3. Yesterday, I took my little brother to the park.

4. He frequently helps his mother with dishes.

5. Carefully carry the milk to the table, please.

Choose three adverbs. Use each one in a sentence. Circle the adverbs.

6. _____

_____

7. _____

_____

8. _____

_____

Use a relative adverb to complete each sentence.

9. Mom wants me to attend school _____ the teachers are outstanding.

10. Jaelynn asked me _____ I was late to practice.

11. Is there a good bakery _____ I can get a cupcake for Dad's birthday?

12. Fiona needs to tell Evan _____ she will help him with his homework.

13. Mr. Rizzo couldn't figure out _____ the students were being so loud.

Choose three relative adverbs. Use each one in a sentence. Circle the relative adverbs.

14. _____

_____

15. _____

_____

16. _____

Progressive Verb Tense

Circle the progressive verbs in each sentence.

1. Mrs. Yu is going to give us homework every day this week.

2. Elizabeth will be asking her mother if we can spend the night.

3. Andrew was practicing his batting for the game tomorrow.

4. They are helping the janitors clean the classroom.

5. Alicia had been walking home from school each afternoon.

6. Mr. Walsh was happy with how hard we were studying.

7. I am planning a birthday surprise for Mom.

Write the correct progressive verb tense form.

8. The Superstars _____ the Tornadoes in the championship.
    (future: play)

9. My baby sister _____ me awake each night with her crying.
    (past: keep)

10. India _____ in a short race today and thinks she might win.
    (present: run)

Write one sentence each using past, present, and future progressive verb tense.

11. _____

_____

12. _____

_____

13. _____

_____

Modal Auxiliary Verbs

Circle the modal verb in each sentence. Then, underline the action verb.

1. Delinda's mom said she might leave practice early today.

2. Iman can roller-skate better than anyone else in the rink.

3. Jason would help Mrs. Petrov if he didn't have to babysit his brother.

4. Our teacher told us we should spend at least 30 minutes each night reading.

5. Watching the final performer could make us late to dinner.

6. You should pack a sweater because it may snow later tonight.

7. Dad said I must eat my dinner before I have dessert.

8. Matthew couldn't play in the game since he broke his wrist.

9. Luke won't help Sasha study because she refused to share her lunch.

10. You shouldn't swim when it is storming outside.

Complete each sentence with a modal verb.

11. Mrs. Perez said we _____ pass the test as long as we study.

12. Mom _____ let me stay up late because of my trip early tomorrow morning.

13. Orlando, Florida, _____ be very hot in July.

14. I can tell by looking at the sky that it _____ rain later today.

15. Mom _____ be very happy to hear that I won the spelling bee at school today!

16. Norris _____ be at school today because he has been sick to his stomach all night.

17. Ginny wanted to know if I _____ play basketball this weekend.

18. Donna planned to leave early but _____ because she was the last person finished.

19. Because of the tropical storm, we _____ lose power.

20. I _____ go to the movies because I had a project to finish.

Name _____ Date _____

Adjectives

Circle the adjectives in each sentence.

1. Courtney has a small, red purse that she carries everywhere.

2. It was a cold, snowy day so I needed my warm, fur-lined boots.

3. Dominique said the concert was loud, so my grandmother shouldn't attend.

4. My dad brought home some beautiful pink flowers.

5. I walked in to the wonderful aroma of fresh-baked cookies.

Place each pair of adjectives in the correct order.

6. Ashton's mom bought him a _____, _____ coat.
　　　　　　　　　　　　　　　　(black, new)

7. Amira baked _____ _____ cakes.
　　　　　　　　　　　　(chocolate, three)

8. Erica wore a _____ _____ dress for picture day.
　　　　　　　　　(cotton, pink)

9. I used _____, _____ triangles on the poster I was making.
　　　　　　　(large, purple)

10. When we were at the garage sale, my mom noticed a

_____ _____ lamp.
　　　(beautiful, glass)

Think of at least three adjectives that could describe each noun below and write them in the correct order. Include proper punctuation.

11. _____ dog

12. _____ storm

13. _____ baby

14. _____ shirt

15. _____ teacher

Prepositional Phrases

Circle the prepositional phrase(s) and underline the preposition(s) in each sentence.

1. I left my book inside my desk.

2. The baby was crawling around the table.

3. Please place your homework on the table at the front of the room.

4. I dropped my pen and had to reach under my chair to get it.

5. Jayla had to stand between Harry and Dustin when the class lined up to go to lunch.

6. The runner leaped over the hurdles as he ran around the track.

7. Ivy accidentally left her key hanging on her coat hook in the closet at school.

8. Please place the dirty dishes in the sink and wipe off the top of the counter.

9. I quickly ran up the stairs since the elevator was not working.

10. It was easy to see through the window since Mom washed it.

Look around the room. Choose five objects and write sentences describing their location using prepositions.

11. _____

_____

12. _____

_____

13. _____

_____

14. _____

_____

15. _____

_____

Name _____ Date _____

Sentences

Underline the subject once and the predicate twice in each sentence.

1. The black and white puppy hopped up on the couch.

2. Hunter and Graham took Jimmy to the park after work.

3. Lucy wanted Henry to play a game of cards with her.

4. Mom stopped at the store after her meeting.

5. Blue whales are found in the ocean.

6. The Revolutionary War is an important part of American history.

7. The children outside the house are waiting to go to school.

8. The red-and-white hot air balloon is floating overhead.

9. I want to play outside before I finish my homework.

10. You should not leave your door unlocked when home alone.

Add a subject or a predicate to complete each sentence.

11. _____ play soccer on the weekends.

12. Heather and Grey _____ .

13. Four little kittens _____ .

14. My teacher _____ .

15. _____ bounced up and down with happiness!

16. The giant, scary beast _____ .

17. _____ were very scared because of the storm.

18. _____ went to the pool and swam all afternoon.

19. Farmers and ranchers _____ .

20. _____ learned how to cook hot dogs.

Fragments and Run-On Sentences

Write **S** for sentence, **F** for fragment, or **R** for run-on.

_____ **1.** The boy asked his mom for cake.

_____ **2.** At the end of recess.

_____ **3.** Ian ran.

_____ **4.** I went to the park I played on the slide.

_____ **5.** Will you help me with my chores?

_____ **6.** Several students not doing homework regularly.

_____ **7.** The storm was bad it blew over a tree.

_____ **8.** Helping my parents and cleaning my room.

Read each sentence below. If it is correct, do nothing. If it is incorrect, rewrite it correctly on the line.

9. I bought a sandwich it was very good.

_____

10. The fireman's coat and boots.

_____

11. Please grab your backpack off the back of the door.

_____

12. After school on Mondays and Wednesdays.

_____

13. Zack went to the store he got a new book.

_____

14. Running a race on Saturday.

_____

15. I ate my dinner, and then I brushed my teeth.

_____

Capitalization

Rewrite each sentence using correct capitalization.

1. detroit is the largest city in michigan.

_____

2. dylan and denise are in fourth grade at shady elementary school.

_____

3. mom and i were both born in august.

_____

4. my family is going to chicago, illinois, to visit my aunt and uncle.

_____

5. the hamilton library has a copy of *the phantom tollbooth*.

_____

6. our class is having our valentine's day celebration at chadwick park.

_____

7. we bought our puppy princess at regency pet store.

_____

8. Read the paragraph. Circle each word that should be capitalized and is not. Place an **X** on each word that is capitalized but should not be.

    I am very excited about thanksgiving. My parents are taking my Brother and me to new york city! we get to travel on a train. we will board the Train in washington, dc. it will only take three hours to get to grand central station. Once we arrive, we are going to check into our hotel and go to central park. There is a Zoo there that my mom went to when she was a little girl. next, we plan to take a carriage ride. i am packing warm clothes because it is chilly there in november. After we finish the ride, we get to walk around times square and eat dinner. I hope we see someone famous! dad said we get to stay up late so we can see all the bright lights. On thursday morning we are going to the thanksgiving day parade. I cannot wait to see all the marching bands and balloons! it will definitely be a trip to remember.

Name _____ Date _____

Quotations

Read the following sentences. Add commas and quotation marks where needed.

1. Mom said Please put on your shoes and jacket so we can leave.

2. Is it OK to play outside today? asked Monique.

3. The park is too far away to walk to said Lee. Let's ride our bikes.

4. After kicking the soccer ball, Pedro yelled Watch out Morgan!

5. Can Evelyn come with us to the movies Mom Felicia asked.

6. I love my new puppy said Avery. He is so cute!

7. Mom, can we play outside after dinner? asked Brady.

8. Jenna screamed Look out Forrest!

Write at least four lines of dialogue between two characters. Be sure to use correct punctuation.

_____
_____
_____
_____
_____
_____
_____
_____
_____
_____
_____
_____

Coordinating Conjunctions

Write the correct coordinating conjunction in each sentence.

1. Jill can play the piano _____ she can't play the violin.

2. Mrs. Peters doesn't want us to forget our homework, _____ she reminds us every day before we leave.

3. I looked everywhere in the classroom, _____ I couldn't find my pencil.

4. We can go to the park, _____ we can play video games at home.

5. Mom said Mariah has to do her homework, _____ she needs to clean her room.

6. Madison felt like she had run for miles, _____ she was nowhere near the finish line.

7. David is amazing at basketball, _____ he doesn't like to play.

8. I want to run in the Labor Day race, _____ I want to finish in first place.

Use a coordinating conjunction to combine each set of sentences.

9. Paul likes to listen to music. Paul likes to play video games.

_____

10. We should lock the door before we leave. I don't have a key to the house.

_____

11. I want to go to my friend's house. I must do my homework first.

_____

12. Leo doesn't like doing puzzles. Leo doesn't like playing games.

_____

13. I looked inside my desk. I could not find my book.

_____

14. Nikki raked her neighbor's leaves. The neighbor paid her 20 dollars.

_____

15. Kristen was very nervous. Kristen stood up to the bully.

_____

Homophones and Homographs

Circle the correct homophone(s) in each sentence.

1. Jamal got (to, too, two) pencils (for, four) his little brother.

2. Frederico had a (peace, piece) of chocolate cake for dessert.

3. When Evelyn was hiking in the woods, she got to (sea, see) many (dear, deer).

4. Erin wants to (right, write) a letter to her (ant, aunt).

5. Gerardo's mom (cent, sent) him lots of (mail, male) while he was at summer camp.

6. Erik asked (which, witch) (road, rode) Casey lived on.

7. Isabella's team (one, won) the final game (buy, by) only a few points.

8. Mrs. Dumon is taking us to the (fair, fare) on Saturday.

9. Do you (know, no) how many (hours, ours) we spend at school each year?

10. I helped my mom measure the (flour, flower) for the cake.

Illustrate each sentence in order to show the correct meanings of the homographs.

The bat was holding a bat.	The plate will sink to the bottom of the sink.
The little girl with the bow on her head will bow.	The boy had a tear in his eye because his paper began to tear.

Greek and Latin Affixes and Roots

Look at the chart. Read each affix or root and its definition. Think of a word you know that includes that affix or root. Write it in the appropriate column. Then, write a short definition of the word.

Affix or Root	Meaning	Example Word	Definition
bio	life		
geo	earth		
phon	sound		
auto	self		
tele	distant		
-ful	full of		
-ness	quality of being		
-ology	study of		
mis-	without		
anti-	against		
-able	can be done		
graph	related to writing		

Antonyms and Synonyms

Read each row of words. Circle the words that are synonyms.

1.	large	gigantic	huge	small
2.	beautiful	pretty	sweet	happy
3.	angry	irritated	excited	mad
4.	subtract	add	combine	take
5.	walk	run	sprint	crawl

Read each row of words. Circle the words that are antonyms.

6.	stay	leave	keep	walk
7.	dark	night	bright	sun
8.	gift	give	take	place
9.	short	large	tall	man
10.	stand	crawl	fast	slow

Complete the chart.

Synonym		Antonym
	small	
	sad	
	dark	
	warm	
	tall	
	happy	
	nice	

Figurative Language

Match each proverb and adage to its intended meaning.

1. The grass is always greener on the other side of the fence.

2. The squeaky wheel gets greased.

3. Absence makes the heart grow fonder.

4. Beauty is in the eye of the beholder.

5. Birds of a feather flock together.

6. Two wrongs don't make a right.

7. You can't have your cake and eat it too.

8. Two heads are better than one.

9. Look before you leap.

10. Stop and smell the roses.

A. You feel more affection towards someone when you are not with them.

B. The loudest problems are the ones that usually get the attention.

C. Take time to enjoy life.

D. People often think other people have it better than they do.

E. It is helpful to get someone else's advice.

F. If someone does something bad to you, don't do anything bad in response.

G. Each person has their own idea of what is beautiful.

H. Before you do something, consider the consequences.

I. People who like the same things are typically friends.

J. Doing two good things at once is not possible.

Complete the chart.

	Example	Type of Figurative Language	Meaning
11.	That test was a piece of cake!		
12.	My sister runs like lightning.		
13.	The flowers are ballerinas in the wind.		
14.	My brother is as slow as a snail in the morning.		
15.	He's a volcano ready to explode!		
16.	Summer in Texas is a blazing bonfire.		
17.	It's raining cats and dogs right now.		

Context Clues

Many words have more than one meaning. Read each sentence. Use context clues to circle the correct definition of the bolded word.

1. The boat had trouble getting through the **channel**.

  focus   body of water   to direct

2. After singing in the talent show, Kennedy took a **bow**.

  bending of the body   a ribbon   front of a boat

3. That test was so long I could hardly **bear** it.

  an animal   endure   support

4. Even though Linden was teasing him, Mason kept his **cool**.

  self-control   low temperature   awesome

5. During the race, Nina had the **lead** the whole way.

  show the way   first place   be in charge

Read each sentence. Circle the meaning of the bolded word. Underline the clues that helped you determine the meaning.

6. I bought a new shirt because it was a great **bargain**.

  beautiful fabric   colorful design

  good price   excellent fit

7. When Mrs. Smith was sick, she went to the doctor hoping he would give her a **remedy**.

  appointment   cure

  medicine   explanation

8. The storm was **severe** and left many people without power.

  very bad   windy

  wet   loud

9. After running five miles, Joseph was very **weary**.

  excited   ready

  hungry   tired

10. Holding the door for someone is a wonderful **gesture**.

  nice idea   hand movement

  loud noise   compliment

A

What is a relative pronoun?

_____

List at least three examples.

_____

_____

_____

B

Write two sentences using relative pronouns. Circle the relative pronoun in each sentence.

_____

_____

_____

_____

C

Write *who*, *that*, *which*, or *whose* to complete each sentence.

He wanted to know _____ book this was.

He wanted to know _____ to give the book to.

He wanted to know _____ book to read.
He wanted to know what to do with

_____ book.

D

List three examples of adverbs.

_____ _____ _____

Use one in a sentence.

_____

_____

_____

E

List three relative adverbs.

_____ _____ _____

Use one in a sentence.

_____

_____

_____

F

Write a sentence from the text that uses vivid verbs to show action.

_____

_____

Rewrite it with a progressive verb tense.

_____

_____

G

Write two sentences using the progressive verb tense for *walk*.

_____

_____

_____

_____

H

Label each verb phrase with **P** for past, **PR** for present, or **F** for future progressive.

_____ is dancing

_____ will be singing

_____ was running

Write two sentences about school using modal verbs. Circle the modal verbs.

_____

_____

_____

_____

I

Complete each sentence with a modal verb.

When it is lightning you _____ not swim.

I know how to play, so I _____ help you.

He asked if I _____ play soccer.

If I do not do my homework, I _____ be in trouble.

J

Number the following from 1 to 8 to show the correct order for placing adjectives.

_____ color   _____ origin

_____ age   _____ opinion

_____ material   _____ purpose

_____ size   _____ shape

K

Place the adjectives and noun in the correct order.

little   puppies   gray   six

_____

three   triangles   orange   large

_____

L

Write at least two adjectives in the correct order before each noun.

_____ flower

_____ game

_____ baby

_____ cookies

M

Describe your classroom using at least four adjectives.

_____

_____

_____

_____

_____

N

Use a preposition to complete each sentence.

Place your math book _____ your desk.

The dog circled _____ the cat.

The bunny hopped _____ the hole.

I stood _____ Lisa in line.

O

Write two sentences using prepositional phrases to describe your bedroom.

_____

_____

_____

_____

P

Label each sentence **S** for sentence, **F** for fragment, or **R** for run-on.

_____ Brooke ran home quickly after school.

_____ After eating too much food all weekend.

_____ Taking tests is so hard.

_____ We played soccer the other team won.

Q

Turn each fragment into a complete sentence.
Yesterday when I got home.

_____

_____

My brother Abraham, who is six years old.

_____

_____

R

Correct each run-on sentence.
Last week we played soccer, two students got hurt.

_____

_____

I love to play soccer my team usually wins.

_____

_____

S

Write **C** for correct or **I** for incorrect.

_____ Can you get that for me asked Mrs. Wolf.

_____ "Please!" begged Perry. "I really want to go!"

_____ "I really don't want to clean up," complained Nona.

_____ "Let's win this game! Exclaimed Patrick."

T

Add the missing punctuation to each sentence.

Mom asked if I wanted to get ice cream after dinner

Don't forget your shirt Mom yelled

I think Nathan is playing in the game on Saturday answered Dad

U

List at least four reasons a word should be capitalized:

_____

_____

_____

_____

V

Circle the letters that should be capitalized.

miguel was born in detroit, michigan, on february 3, 2005.
my brothers and i go to washington elementary school.
pilar's favorite book is _charlotte's web._
we celebrate thanksgiving on the fourth thursday of november.

W

Write a complete sentence that contains two capital letters in addition to the first word.

_____

_____

_____

_____

X

Complete each definition.

Homophones are words that _____

_____ .

Homographs are words that _____

_____ .

Y

Write a set of homophones and illustrate them to show the difference.

Z

Find homographs in a text. List them below.

_____ _____

_____ _____

_____ _____

_____ _____

AA

Write **S** for simile, **M** for metaphor, or **I** for idiom.

_____ It's raining cats and dogs out there!

_____ The winter ground was a blanket of snow.

_____ She's as pretty as a summer sunset.

_____ What's the matter—does the cat have your tongue?

AB

Finish each simile.

She is as fast as _____ .

The baby is as loud as _____ .

He sings like _____ .

That woman is as slow as _____ .

AC

List one example of figurative language from the text.

_____

What does it mean?

_____

_____

AD

Write one word in the text that you did not

know. _____

I think it means _____ .

The context clues that helped me are:

_____

_____

AE

Write four words from the text with affixes and roots. Circle the affixes and underline the roots.

_____

_____

_____

_____

AF

Answer Key

Page 9
1. third person; Check students' work. 2. He did not have one. 3. Answers will vary. 4. "Where there's a will, there's a way." If you want something bad enough, you will find a way to get it. 5–6. Answers will vary.

Page 10
1. third person; Check students' work. 2. He was hungry. 3. Answers will vary. 4. He flew like a bullet. He ran quickly. 5–6. Answers will vary.

Page 15
1–3. Answers will vary. 4. Her neighbors took care of her and cared about her.

Page 16
1–3. Answers will vary. 4. the best

Page 17
1–2. Answers will vary. 3–4. Answers will vary. Check students' work.

Page 18
1. Answers will vary. 2. Answers will vary but should include Connor offering to teach David about swimming. 3. Check students' work. Answers will vary. 4. Answers will vary but should include David's inability to swim.

Page 19
1. first person; Check students' work. 2. last minute, quickly; The lunch was gone and the narrator had to quickly make lunch and get to school. 3. She talks to the brothers and then to Dad. 4. Answers will vary.

Page 20
1. Crow and the dog both lose food when they open their mouths. 2. Fox tricked Crow, but the dog lost the bone because of his own greed. 3. Answers will vary. 4. Answers will vary but should include feeling upset over losing her food. 5. better than anyone else's

Page 21
1. excited; new classes, new teachers, and a new junior basketball team; 2. nervous; It will be his first year in middle school. 3. They are brothers and are close. 4. Answers will vary but should include not wanting to go to school at first and then being excited.

Page 22
1. scared; heart beating like a drum and wicked shadows; 2–3. Answers will vary. 4. Check students' work. 5. Answers will vary but should include helping the reader to picture the shadows.

Pages 23–24
A–C. Answers will vary. D. (top to bottom, from the left) D, P, P, PR, PR or D, D, P, PR, PR, PR; E–P. Answers will vary.

Page 25
1. the importance of tipis and how they are made; 2. Answers will vary. 3. They needed homes that could easily be moved. 4. Answers will vary but should include that they are long and straight.

Page 26
1. what the trip on the *Mayflower* was like and how difficult travel and settling in was; 2. Answers will vary. 3. descriptive; Check students' work. 4. how hard it was to make homes in the new land

Page 31
1–2. Answers will vary. 3. disappeared; She was never heard from again. 4. She has never been found but people still talk about her and are still looking for her plane.

Page 32
1. It was interesting. 2. He gives examples of interesting ways people cleaned their teeth. 3. It scrapes off the plaque that your toothbrush cannot get to. 4. Answers will vary.

Answer Key

Page 33
1. Many ancient cultures had interesting explanations for earthquakes. 2. Native Americans and Indians both believed that animals caused earthquakes. Native Americans believe it was a giant sea turtle, whereas Indians thought it was elephants standing on a turtle, which was standing on a snake.
3. Answers will vary but should include the idea of doing something wrong. Answers will vary.
4. descriptive or comparison/contrast;
5. Answers will vary.

Page 34
1. forked; 2. to help the reader visualize the tongue; 3. because a rattlesnake is dangerous and the noise of its tail is a warning; 4. an illustration; 5. It shows the reader what a rattlesnake's tongue and tail look like, which helps when reading about both features. 6. It helps the rattlesnake to know when a predator is nearby since it cannot hear.

Page 35
1. The medulla takes care of all involuntary actions. 2. The cerebellum controls all voluntary actions. 3. The cerebrum controls voluntary mental operations and is made up of two hemispheres. 4–6. Answers will vary.
7. Answers will vary but should address the thinking, learning, and memory functions of the cerebrum.

Page 36
1. exact or specific; 2. question and answer;
3. The Dewey Decimal system is a way to organize books in a library so that people will know exactly where to find books they are interested in. 4. the 600s; 5. Answers will vary but should have something to do with science.

Page 37
1. watched; 2. chronological order; 3. Sir Isaac Newton had a rough childhood, but he was able to work hard and discovered gravity.
4. His father died and his mother's new husband did not want Isaac, so he had to live with his grandmother. 5. Answers will vary but should include how hard he worked and how much thinking he did.

Page 38
1. small or little; 2. Answers will vary. 3. Earth's magnetic field; 4. the cause of the northern lights; 5. Answers will vary.

Page 53
The Mysterious Light: 1. her aunt and uncle's farmhouse; 2. visiting France; 3. her uncle's flashlight; 4. in case she had to run for help *A Family Hike*: 1. hiking in the mountains;
2. Answers will vary. 3. teach; 4. every summer; *Insects in Winter*: 1. dig deep in the ground; 2. gather into a ball; 3. the cold weather; 4. ladybugs; *Wolves*: 1. Answers will vary but may include meat eaters, predators, or hunters. 2. meat; 3. their homes are disappearing and they are hunted; 4. They help to balance nature by hunting weak animals. *The Miller's Daughter*: 1. Answers will vary.
2. in a chair; 3. an old silver cup; 4. summer

Page 54
A–H. Answers will vary.

Answer Key

Page 59

Last week I **went** to my aunt's house. It was my cousin's birthday and they were **having** a party to celebrate. She was turning **four** and wanted a princess party**.** **I** was asked to be the prince. At first**,** I didn't want **to** do it**,** but then my **u**ncle called me and **offered** to take me to a basketball game if I did. **When** I arrived**,** my cousin ran up and jumped in my arms. Most of her **friends** were already **there**. Aunt **Heather** had gotten a crown and a purple robe for me to **wear**. I quickly dressed and **joined** the girls in the backyard. I helped them paint **their** nails and then create their own **crowns**. After Jessica opened her gifts**,** it was time for cake. She had picked out a pink, square **one** with purple flowers on top. After everyone left, Jessica crawled into my lap and hugged me. She was so tired, she fell asleep. After I laid her down, **I drove** home. The party **wasn't** nearly as bad as I thought it would be.

Page 60

Carter and Nick have **been** friends for their **entire** lives. They live next **door** to each other and are in **the** same class at school. Both boys have **two** younger sisters and one older brother**. T**hey even play on the same baseball team. When they **meet** someone new**,** they like to pretend they are twins**. Their** parents let them **do homework together every afternoon**. As soon as they finish, they run outside and play until it is time for **dinner**. **Unfortunately**, **C**arter just found out he is **moving** away. **His dad** got a new job in another state. **Their** parents have **talked** and decided that the boys can visit each other every summer **for** two weeks. They have also set up email accounts and can **write** each other every day. They **know** it won't be the same, but they plan to remain friends forever!

Pages 61–62

A–P. Answers will vary.

Page 63

1. pronoun; 2. preposition; 3. modal verb; 4. is baking; 5. will be studying; 6. buy; 7. hear; 8. won; 9. S; 10. F; 11. R; 12. where; 13. why; 14. who; 15. whose; 16. She was sighing at her pesky brother.

Page 64

1. preposition; 2. pronoun; 3. adverb; 4. were cheering; 5. am going to spend; 6. It's; 7. for; 8. knew; new; 9. R; 10. S; 11. F; 12. when; 13. where; 14. whomever; 15. which; 16. I was jumping rope with my friend.

Page 65

1. I; 2. I; 3. C; 4. I; 5. I; 6. C; 7. I; 8. "Do you want spaghetti for dinner?" asked Dad. 9. "I can't believe we won $1,000!" screamed Byron. 10. "Please clean your room," requested Mom. "Then you can play games." 11. I know you want to watch TV, but first you must finish your chores. 12. Last night's snow broke all previous records, and school will be closed for days because of the storm. 13. Jawan moved to Austin, Texas, from Los Angeles, California. 14. Mr. Lee said, "Please clear your desks and take out two pencils." 15. "I can't wait to go to middle school!" exclaimed Myong. "It is going to be so much fun!"

Last weekend**,** my parents **took** us to **N**ew **Y**ork **C**ity. We had such a **great** time**. I** got **to** visit a toy store and my dad bought us **a** new game. We **rode** in a yellow cab**. M**om wanted to visit the zoo. **There** were a bunch of **new** baby elephants. They were so cute! After the zoo**,** we ate hot dogs **from** a food cart**. T**hen we took the subway. I can't imagine having more fun **anywhere**. When my parents **asked** me where we should go next, I told them **O**rlando**, F**lorida. I **hear** there's a mouse there I can **meet**!

Answer Key

Page 66

1. C; 2. I; 3. I; 4. C; 5. I; 6. C; 7. I; 8. "Libby is coming over after dinner," said Mom. 9. "That was the best roller coaster ever!" exclaimed Owen. 10. "We need to take our test," stated Mrs. Foster. "Then, we can have recess." 11. We spent all morning going from one garage sale to the next, and then my mom took me out to lunch at my favorite restaurant. 12. I wanted to study for our spelling test at Paige's house, but my mom made me stay home and work on my math homework with Dad. 13. My mom got a new job, so we will be moving from Detroit, Michigan, to Atlanta, Georgia. 14. Mr. Martinez asked, "Would you like to take the attendance to the office?" 15. "Our team won the semi-final game," explained Luke. "That means we are in the championship game."

Macon Silva lives in **D**allas**, T**exas. His younger sister is **two** years old**. S**he follows him everywhere he **goes**. Most kids would find that annoying. Not **M**acon. He adores his little sister! **H**e was twelve years old when she **was** born. He wished for a brother**,** but his mom always said "If wishes were horses, dreamers would ride." He wasn't sure what that meant, but he **knew** he didn't care. Olivia giggles at everything and is **a lot** of fun! Macon can't wait to watch her grow up.

Page 67

1. angry; 2. leaves; 3. scared; 4–9. Check students' work. 10. overactive; 11. to lead wrongly; 12. never come to an end; 13–16. Answers will vary.

Page 68

1. excited; 2. harmful; 3. pleasant; 4–9. Check students' work. 10. small scope; 11. to heat again; 12. to not be alert; 13–16. Check students' work.

Page 71

1. which of you; 2. who won the tournament; 3. that I read; 4. that everyone likes; 5. whomever I wanted; 6. that my father made for dinner; 7. whichever cookie you want; 8. whose backpack this is; 9. Whose paper; 10. whoever wins the spelling bee; 11–17. Answers will vary.

Page 72

1. quickly; 2. often; 3. Yesterday; 4. frequently; 5. Carefully; 6–16. Answers will vary. Check students' work.

Page 73

1. is going to give; 2. will be asking; 3. was practicing; 4. are helping; 5. had been walking; 6. were studying; 7. am planning; 8. will be playing; 9. was keeping; 10. is running; 11–13. Answers will vary.

Page 74

1. might leave; 2. can roller-skate; 3. would help; 4. should spend; 5. could make; 6. should pack; may snow; 7. must eat; 8. couldn't play; 9. won't help; 10. shouldn't swim; 11–20. Answers will vary but should make sense.

Page 75

1. small, red; 2. cold, snowy; warm, fur-lined; 3. loud; 4. beautiful, pink; 5. wonderful; fresh-baked; 6. new, black; 7. three chocolate; 8. pink cotton; 9. large, purple; 10. beautiful glass; 11–15. Answers will vary.

Page 76

1. inside my desk; 2. around the table; 3. on the table, at the front, of the room; 4. under my chair; 5. between Harry and Dustin; 6. over the hurdles, around the track; 7. on her coat hook, in the closet, at school; 8. in the sink, of the counter; 9. up the stairs; 10. through the window; 11–15. Answers will vary.

© Carson-Dellosa • CD-104944

Answer Key

Page 77

1. The black and white puppy/hopped up on the couch. 2. Hunter and Graham/took Jimmy to the park after work. 3. Lucy/wanted Henry to play a game of cards with her. 4. Mom/stopped at the store after her meeting.
5. Blue whales/are found in the ocean. 6. The Revolutionary War/is an important part of American history. 7. The children outside the house/are waiting to go to school. 8. The red-and-white hot air balloon/is floating overhead. 9. I/want to play outside before I finish my homework. 10. You/should not leave your door unlocked when home alone.
11–20. Answers will vary.

Page 78

1. S; 2. F; 3. S; 4. R; 5. S; 6. F; 7. R; 8. F;
9. I bought a sandwich. It was very good.
10. Answers will vary. 11. correct;
12. Answers will vary. 13. Zack went to the store. He got a new book. 14. Answers will vary. 15. correct

Page 79

1. Detroit is the largest city in Michigan.
2. Dylan and Denise are in fourth grade at Shady Elementary School. 3. Mom and I were both born in August. 4. My family is going to Chicago, Illinois, to visit my aunt and uncle.
5. The Hamilton Library has a copy of *The Phantom Tollbooth*. 6. Our class is having our Valentine's Day celebration at Chadwick Park. 7. We bought our puppy Princess at Regency Pet Store. 8. circled: I, Thanksgiving, New York City, We, We, Washington, DC; It, Grand Central Station, Central Park, Next, I, November, Times Square, Dad, Thursday, Thanksgiving Day, It; X: brother, train, zoo

Page 80

1. Mom said, "Please put on your shoes and jacket so we can leave." 2. "Is it OK to play outside today?" asked Monique. 3. "The park is too far away to walk to," said Lee. "Let's ride our bikes." 4. After kicking the soccer ball, Pedro yelled, "Watch out, Morgan!" 5. "Can Evelyn come with us to the movies, Mom?" Felicia asked. 6. "I love my new puppy," said Avery. "He is so cute!" 7. "Mom, can we play outside after dinner?" asked Brady. 8. Jenna screamed, "Look out, Forrest!"
Answers will vary.

Page 81

1. but; 2. so; 3. but; 4. or; 5. and; 6. but;
7. but; 8. and; 9. Paul likes to listen to music, and he likes to play video games. 10. We should lock the door before we leave, but I don't have a key to the house. 11. I want to go to my friend's house, but I must do my homework first. 12. Leo doesn't like doing puzzles or playing games. 13. I looked inside my desk, but I could not find my book.
14. Nikki raked her neighbor's leaves, so the neighbor paid her 20 dollars. 15. Kristen was very nervous, but she stood up to the bully.

Page 82

1. two, for; 2. piece; 3. see, deer; 4. write, aunt; 5. sent, mail; 6. which, road; 7. won, by; 8. fair; 9. know, hours; 10. flour; Check students' work.

Page 83

Answers will vary.

Page 84

1. large, gigantic, huge; 2. beautiful, pretty;
3. angry, irritated, mad; 4. add, combine;
5. run, sprint; 6. stay, leave; 7. dark, bright;
8. give, take; 9. short, tall; 10. fast, slow;
Answers will vary.

Answer Key

Page 85

1. D; 2. B; 3. A; 4. G; 5. I; 6. F; 7. J; 8. E;
9. H; 10. C; 11. metaphor; The test was easy.
12. simile; She is fast. 13. metaphor; The
flowers are swaying back and forth. 14. simile;
He is very slow. 15. metaphor; He is extremely
angry. 16. metaphor; It is very hot. 17. idiom;
It's raining hard.

Page 86

1. body of water; 2. bending of the body;
3. endure; 4. self-control; 5. first place;
6. good price; Check students' work.
7. medicine; Check students' work. 8. very
bad; Check students' work. 9. tired; Check
students' work. 10. nice idea; Check students'
work.

Pages 87–90

A. a pronoun that introduces a relative clause;
Answers will vary. B. Answers will vary. Check
students' work. C. whose; who; which; that;
D–G. Answers will vary. H. PR, F, P; I. Answers
will vary. Check students' work. J. Answers will
vary. K. color = 5; age = 3; material = 7; size
= 2; origin = 6; opinion = 1; purpose = 8;
shape = 4; L. six little gray puppies; three large
orange triangles; M–P. Answers will vary; Q. S,
F, S, R; R–S. Answers will vary. T. I, C, C; I;
U. Mom asked if I wanted to get ice cream after
dinner. "Don't forget your shirt!" Mom yelled.
"I think Nathan is playing in the game on
Saturday," answered Dad. V. Answers will vary
but may include: I, titles, beginning of sentence,
days of the week, months of the year, names,
proper nouns; W. Miguel; Detroit, Michigan;
February; My; I; Washington; Elementary;
School; Pilar's; *Charlotte's; Web*; We;
Thanksgiving; Thursday; November; X. Answers
will vary. Y. words that are pronounced the
same but have different meanings; words
that are spelled the same but have different
meanings and may be pronounced differently;
Z–AA. Answers will vary. AB. I, M, S, I;
AC–AF. Answers will vary.